TRUE WORSHIP

The Gateway to Intimacy with God

BRYAN T. WILLIAMS

Absolute Author
Publishing House

True Worship: The Gateway to Intimacy with God
Copyright © 2020 Bryan T. Williams, Pittsburgh, Pa.

For permissions, please contact: Bryan Williams, zapcenter12@gmail.com.

Edited by Best selling author and editor Annie Jenkinson

Cover design and page formatting completed by Richell Balansag

---

All rights reserved. No portion of this book may be reproduced in any form without permission from the publisher, except as permitted by U.S. copyright law or in the form of a short quotation within a book review or similar.

ISBN: Paperback 978-1-64953-176-6
ISBN: Digital Version 978-1-64953-177-3

DEDICATIONS

Thank you Jesus!

For Mom – Your tireless example throughout years of trial shows me Jesus. You are a treasure.

My wife Melissa – What a praise and worship warrior you are! I pray Gods intimate blessings continue to flow into your life. You always give me the love, encouragement, and time needed to keep plugging away at completing this work. Thank you so much! I love you.

The Para-Church Fellowship – My brothers in Christ, ministers of the Gospel, and the most dedicated men of God that I know: Harlan Humphrey, Keith Cash, Ron Markel, Doug Williams, John Walker, and of course, my main man, Michael Heiman. We sharpen our iron against each other, minister to one another, and hold each other accountable with Godly counsel. I love you guys.

CONTENTS

Introduction 7
Chapter One: Attaining Focus 15
Chapter Two: 2 Timothy 2:15 20
Chapter Three: John 4 27
Chapter Four: The Meaning of 'Must' 30
Chapter Five: 'Seeketh/Seeks' 32
Chapter Six: 'True' 40
Chapter Seven: What is a Worshiper? 47
Chapter Eight: Worship 65
Chapter Nine: 'In Spirit/Spirit' 77
Chapter Ten: The Tabernacle of Moses 86
Chapter Eleven: Worship and His Presence 106
Chapter Twelve: A Desperate Woman 126
Chapter Thirteen: A Worship Experience 130
Chapter Fourteen: Worship and Faith 137
Chapter Fifteen: Worship and Brokenness 144

Chapter Sixteen: Worship and Dying to Self 164

Chapter Seventeen: Worship: the Realm of Miracles 176

Chapter Eighteen: True Worship:
The Gateway to Intimacy with God 186

References 193

INTRODUCTION

Have you ever had what you would describe as a truly breathtaking moment?

Most of us have.

Are you able to go back in your mind and re-live that experience?

Take a moment and try. Really think hard and try to transport yourself back there.

Attempt to describe it to yourself.

What exactly did you experience? How did you feel? What were you thinking while the event was taking place? What emotions went through your mind and heart?

Some people I have asked this question have described events as simple as looking up into a cloudless night sky while on vacation in a different part of the world, marveling at the vault of stars rotating above them, stars they had never seen before.

Others stated that they had this type of breathtaking experience as they took in the first glimpses of their only child being born, or when they were finally able to walk outside and smell the flowers again after being ill and bed-ridden for a long period.

Of course, your breathtaking experience will be one that's uniquely personal to you, and your interpretation of what is breathtaking will differ from anyone else's.

So, it's fair to say I've heard many diverse responses to this question over the years when presenting this topic. And every recollection seems filled with wonder!

INTRODUCTION

Every experience *was* breathtaking.

You see, there are no right or wrong answers to this question; it's not a trick question, just an attempt to help you remember a time or event that you felt blew you away with its grandeur or splendor.

Most of the stories I hear when I ask this are amazingly good.

Others, not so much.

Though not often described in the same manner, I've heard stories told stemming from extremely negative events too.

Does that surprise you? If so, I can definitely understand that. It surprised me as well.

But in some cases, experiences were described that, while still breathtaking in nature, had the intense gravitas of a devastating situation, maybe even one that became life-changing in its scope as it settled upon the person's life in that moment.

I had always thought of a *breathtaking experience* as something highly pleasurable until then.

But I learned, they aren't always, are they?

Moments don't *have* to be life-changers to be considered either, yet many are. And they all certainly have the power to alter your perceptions of life in that very moment.

Experiences with God can be much the same in many instances. Sometimes, when life seems difficult, we can reach out to Him in desperation—while other times we can experience a quiet reflection with Him. Either way, we find cherished moments in which we can feel His presence more intimately, and it brings home the reality that He is *always* there at our side, even when we are *not* reaching for Him.

Those are always such special times, aren't they?

A friend of mine described one of his special—and quiet—but breathtaking experiences with the Lord.

He lives in Western Pennsylvania but saved up his money and vacation time from his job, to drive out West to hunt antelope. And of course, having worked so hard and saved so avidly to indulge one of his favorite pastimes, he was extremely excited when the time finally came to take that trip.

As he explained it, he was on his trip and one routine night before bedtime, he went outside to do his business in the bushes. He looked up, expecting to see the same cloud-covered sky that he had become accustomed to seeing back in the East. But there, in Big Country, the skies were crystal clear and the air was sharp, and the vast spectacle of space seemed to literally descend upon him. In that moment, a distinct awareness was communicated to his mind that the very same God who had so incredibly created and sustained such a large and expansive universe filled with stars and planets, also now filled—and fills in perpetuity—all the spaces in and throughout it as well! There was *no space* in which God was not! He became astutely aware that God was everywhere, in the great expanses, in the skies, in the vast hillsides and the undulating, verdant valleys, but also in the tiniest spaces, and in the most infinitesimal things. He was present in every small stone, in a leaf, a breath of air, a beetle, a mouse scurrying through the undergrowth, and in every word or thought.

An unimaginable impossibility settled upon him; God really was (and is) *everywhere*!

It was the realization that God was not only permeating the space *between* the stars in the heavens, but *in and through* each heavenly body as well. He was upholding them, binding them all together, the cement that unified everyone and everything. He had heard this said many times before, of course, but it took that beautiful moment of reflection, out there seemingly alone and so at one with nature, to really *realize* what it meant. He let it soak in, finally able to feel that message reach deep within his body and soul.

Now, he saw how God *literally* held all things together, exactly as it stated in Scripture, even extending down to the dusty earth and to the air around him that he and all of God's own creatures breathed in.

Instantly, he *knew* God was there with him in that moment.

INTRODUCTION

He was not alone, and never would be.

The reality of God's omnipresence overwhelmed him. It was more than simply an intellectual stimulation. Yes, his mind was engaged, but so was his heart! My friend more than knew that God was everywhere at that special moment; he actually *felt* Him all around, in and through him, and had a sense that what he was experiencing extended up and throughout the vastness of the universe he beheld above.

"God is everywhere" was a statement he had previously been accustomed to saying, but those words were too trite and underwhelming for who God actually became to him in that moment. And these words—ones that trip so easily off all of our tongues—didn't and couldn't even *begin* to touch the tiniest portion of what God does to sustain not only us, but every part of the universe, every second, of every minute, of every day.

God showed up and revealed the tiniest portion of who He is to my friend, and my friend stood with his mouth agape, quivering in awe. He had just experienced a quiet, yet powerful encounter with God, and he has lived in the reality of that moment ever since. It's a simple awareness that God is always with him in everything he does and everywhere he goes. Holding him. Sustaining him.

It comforts him to know he can simply whisper, and God is there all around him, to hear.

Many of us have had these types of experiences, haven't we? Those quiet, or 'alone times' when God has seemed to reveal Himself to us in a special way that has brought us closer to Him, or that has given clarity concerning who He is. And you live out the rest of your life in the comfort of the revelation He provided. If you are truly a Christian, you have almost certainly had such experiences yourself.

Those moments are incredibly precious.

There are other times where the presence of God totally overwhelms you, and because of the power and intensity of the moment, you may find yourself flattened out on the floor weeping and wailing, as His majesty envelops you! He can come in power, in peace, in joy, in love, in jubilation, and in all His glory! He can come in whatever aspect of His character He desires to reveal to you in that moment.

There are also many times when He will appear to you in Holiness, and at these times, you will feel as if every unclean deed or thought you have ever experienced is arrayed before you. Even those 'good' things that you have done that you considered your 'righteous deeds' fall before Him as a putrid stench in the nostrils of the unimaginably pure and Holy One standing before you.

You actually experience this just like the prophet Isaiah did in his sixth chapter, as he described how being in the Presence of the Lord made him cry out, "Woe is me! For I am undone…"

Yet even then, through your wailing and moaning, when you're laid out on the floor totally bereft of strength, feeling as if somehow you are being completely *unmade*, you find Him gently wiping away the stains of everything that was in your past, and comforting you in His love.

Anytime God's manifested presence enters man's naturally perceived realm, the glory and majesty of who He is can be completely overwhelming both mentally and emotionally.

Ezekiel had many instances with the presence of the Lord, and each time, he said, "I fell at His feet". It then would take the Spirit of the Lord entering into him to pick him back up or give him the strength to stand again. (Eze. 1:28 – 2:1-2, 3:24).

In one instance, (Eze. 3:15), he sat there astonished or overwhelmed for *seven whole days* after experiencing God's presence. Wow! To have been so inundated with God's presence or His message to you that you sit completely overwhelmed for seven days? I can't even *imagine* what that felt like!

And again, Moses spent forty days and nights with the Lord on the mountain, and didn't eat *or* drink anything during that time, having himself entirely sustained by God's presence.

INTRODUCTION

That is incredible! But it gets better! When he came down from the Mount, his face reflected the glory of God in such a way that his skin *visibly* glowed, and he had to wear a veil to cover himself so the People wouldn't be afraid. (Exodus 34:29-33).

Imagine *that*!

These moments of being in God's presence, and many more like them in Scripture, totally overwhelmed the men and women of God.

Some theologians claim that these experiences are exceptions to the rule, and that God doesn't work that way anymore. I've also heard that those experiences were for the prophets of God in *that* day, so they could accomplish whatever plans He had for them to accomplish.

On the one hand, I can't really argue with them. Most of us have been taught that those experiences with God, spoken of by the prophets like Moses, Isaiah, or Ezekiel, *were* as they were either being commissioned, or as they carried out the purposes of God in their lives. And we learn that they were strengthened and encouraged or empowered to continue forward, knowing God was with them after those encounters occurred.

However, on the other hand, I know that I *have* been a part of countless times over the last thirty years, when the Lord has come into intimate communion with me. Some have been times when He has completely blown me away with His vastness and power like He did as He spoke with Job. Other times, it's felt as if He seemed to completely disassemble my very being, until I was *undone*—as Isaiah was.

Many times, the encounter started out as my everyday prayer time, but grew into a totally encompassing intimacy between my Father and me, and although I didn't know it at the time, I found out later that all in my house, even my dogs, sat in hushed awe while being touched in various ways by the presence of God.

I'll describe some of those experiences as we move on.

They all occurred not because anyone was special or individually commissioned and appointed by God for a task. They happened because the decision was made to seek after God with all my heart, and that included giving God the one thing Scripture states that He is looking for.

This is what I now encourage you to do.

This is the purpose of this book.

For now, you need to understand that there is so much more awaiting you.

And it's all contained in a person.

All you need do is reach out and grasp ahold of Him.

CHAPTER ONE

ATTAINING FOCUS

So, I began by asking if you'd ever had a breathtaking experience, such as any kind of natural one?

Well, let's sharpen our focus even more now.

Think again for a moment.

Have you ever had an incredible, or intense *supernatural* experience with God? Not simply a natural moment that managed to take your breath away, but an overwhelming spiritual occurrence in the presence of the true and living God of the universe?

Again, many of you will have had one. Perhaps not like the experience described previously, or those penned within the pages of the Bible, but intense and supernatural, nonetheless. Events and occurrences that you couldn't accredit to anything or anyone other than God.

How did your experience happen?

Can you recall what you were doing when God arrived in your circumstance?

Some have said that God totally overwhelmed them at a time when they did absolutely nothing to ask for it. They weren't in prayer, and they were not fasting, and they felt sure their mind was not even focused upon God at that time. Well, these are fantastic times when the grace of God is sovereignly poured out in that moment, and when God can reveal His plans, nature, character, etc., to you.

Many others I've spoken to over the years have told their stories of times where God arrived while they were in the midst of an incredible time of praising Him. Sometimes, He manifested while they were at church, and other times while they were at home, but every time, He overwhelmed them, intervening in a situation and flooding their soul with peace, wholly changing the atmosphere within the church, the home, etc.

And every time, they were overjoyed! It had so great an impact that they have ever since longed for another experience just like that one.

But let's look at what tends to happen in the majority of Christians after some of these encounters with the presence of God. This becomes our mindset.

Many speak of their Christian experience as if they are a person on a long journey through the scorching heat of a desert. The sun beats down on their weary body until they feel as though they just can't push on any farther. But they know that they have to keep moving, keep pushing. This life is drudgery in the extreme, so we all just have to hold on and trust that when we truly get to the end of our rope and can take no more, God *will* reach down and give us a little more strength to continue trudging through this desert wasteland called life.

You may have also entertained this thought at one time or another.

Is this how you see your interactions with God?

Do you feel that each experience with Him becomes like a long drink of water that sustains you just long enough, and gives you exactly what is needed to make it over to the next tiny watering hole in the desert?

This may, in some instances, likely be your perspective. Let me assure you,

I've been there too.

However, that's *not* how God operates. He wants to become more to you.

Many of us long for more of Him to strengthen us through life, but we just don't know how to get there.

Therefore, we become frustrated, thinking things about God that fit our experiences, but don't fit what the Bible, the Word of God says about Him. Many times, this frustration can turn to anger and we can appear mad at the world. Other times, it rears its head as apathy, where we just give up and start to voice things like, "Well, God is sovereign, so He can do whatever He wants".

But in either instance, we are likely to give up seeking after *more* of Him, because we think He *cannot* be found. He comes and goes as He pleases, does *whatever* He wants, *when* He wants because He's God.

Ever feel this way?

These thoughts and feelings are real, so I'm not making light of them. They have caused many hurts within the body of Christ. But although they may contain nuggets of truth, they are based upon *false assumptions and beliefs* about God.

Hopefully, we can address some of these limiting beliefs while we are on this journey together.

What most people are surprised to learn though, is that what they experienced with God does not have to be something that's only once in a blue moon, or only when times get tough. That's right; you don't have to wait until some future time after you leave this life, to live in intimate communion with the God of the universe.

You can have it now. But only when you begin to give God what He's looking for.

That's right. This is not a one-way street where we take and take from God, but never give Him what He's been seeking.

You'll find those answers—about how to reach God intimately and consistently—as we progress through this study.

So, please open your heart to the truths that you will discover within the pages of this book. They can literally be life-changing if you apply them.

Please understand, just *reading* a book is not enough. Many people read countless books about all manner of subjects, but they'll only become true experts at the subject which they have been reading about, in all its fine detail, when they put it into practice.

It's exactly the same with your relationship with God.

Don't just read this book as you would a textbook, scrolling along looking for identifying pieces of information. Read it deliberately and with the intention of pausing to consider what the Holy Spirit may be saying to your heart in that moment as you read, and please give Him the thought, time, and application He deserves.

Let Him lead you and guide you into *all* truth.

He'll tell you if what is being taught is right or wrong.

You need to truly consider how you can begin welcoming God into your life, every moment of your day, not just waiting for those pivotal moments when you're sure He will simply show up to help you get out of a situation. God should be welcomed into every small moment of your life and woven into *everything* you do!

If you commit to this, you *will* see God's Hand become manifested in your reality. You *will* begin to experience Him in more intimate ways, and those breathtaking experiences we spoke of earlier will become a larger portion of your everyday walk with Him.

The information contained herein has changed lives the world over and brought the people of God into closer communion with their Creator.

This can happen for you too.

Please, let each learned truth, once proven, sink deep into your heart, then put it into the practice of your daily life.

Remember: reading is not enough.

Putting it into practice is the only action that will bring you closer to God. You will find that God will come and commune with you so often and so intimately that your life, your actions, *your very nature* begins transforming into His image like never before, simply from time spent in His presence.

You don't need a seminary degree, or a certain level of intelligence, to achieve this communion with God.

And you don't have to have grown up in the perfect religious home for God to reveal Himself to you and intervene in your life as He's never done before.

You need *nothing but your desire* to see the Face of God.

The real question will be, "Will you take the first step, and give Him what He's looking for?"

CHAPTER TWO

2 TIMOTHY 2:15

2 Timothy 2:15 (KJV) says, "Study to show thyself approved unto God, a workman that needeth not be ashamed, but rightly divides the word of truth..."

In our context, the word 'study' means to exert oneself, endeavor, to give diligence to something. It's showing that God wants *you* to do something instead of sitting dormant and doing nothing with His Word.

You have to study, put in work, exert yourself to understand the true meaning of the Word of God.

This is *not* simply sitting in church, listening to the message, and taking it all in as truth!

That's how deception sneaks into the body of Christ!

This is why so much false doctrine and the traditions of men have spewed forth as truths from our pulpits, creeping into the Church to become a part of our theology.

Yes, part of the blame belongs squarely on the shoulders of the leaders who put forth these falsehoods, but a large portion of the fault also belongs with the body of Christ itself.

We have refused to study the Word of God for ourselves, not taking the time to ascertain what is true or false. Therefore, the masses go away believing as truth everything that is taught from the pulpit as if it were the pure, unadulterated Word of God—when many times, it's simply not.

I'm so glad the Lord placed a man of God in my life, my spiritual mentor whom I refer to as Pops, who gave me an incredible piece of advice I have reiterated many times when I have been teaching.

And now, I give the same advice to you.

"Don't believe a thing I say! In fact, you can't! Scripture gives us all a command to,

> *'Prove all things, hold fast to that which is good!' (1 Thess. 5:21)*

"Prove *all* things…" Pops would continue, "…*all* excludes nothing!"

It is your own responsibility to prove the statements that come out from behind the pulpit, from over the airwaves, or that are whispered into your ears. That means you must prove or disprove what's being taught *before* allowing it to become a part of your thinking. Anywhere and in every instance information comes to your awareness, it should be held with a degree of disbelief until it's proven either correct or incorrect, because the process of proving prevents you from being deceived.

Once it's proven to be the Word of God, to be the unadulterated truth, then you *must* hold fast to that truth, which means applying it and living it in your life. But you *must* go through the process of proving or disproving it first, as there are no shortcuts, no getting around that necessity.

Let's look again at this verse:

> *"Prove all things; hold fast that which is good."*
> *- 1 Thess. 5:21*

The word 'prove' in the Greek means, to try, test, and examine all things. So, this is what you are told to do, and do it you *must*. You owe it to yourself, to others, and to God.

In studying and giving diligence to the understanding of God's Word so you can be approved of God as it states it our main verse, 2 Timothy 2:15, you've got to try, test, and examine all things.

All things, without exception.

In many cases, this means trying and striving to *disprove* them.

Look at other Scriptures and compare them with what it is that you are trying to learn.

Chase down Scriptural references of similar Bible verses, or topics that fit what you are studying. Look at the cultural and historical contexts of what is being said to gain further understanding. There's so much more you can do to prove whether the things you are being taught are Scripturally correct and in accord with the rest of the inspired Word, or not. And should you discover they are not, then you *ought not* try and make them fit just because it may suit you or your life to do so.

The process of proving all things is how you study and exert yourself, endeavoring and giving diligence to finding out the truth of God's Word. This is much of what studying to show yourself approved unto God, entails.

So to recap, you are to study, exert yourself, endeavor, give diligence to proving, testing, or examining *all* things, so that you can show yourself approved unto God, a workman who need not be ashamed, but rightly divides the Word of truth.

Let's look at one more word in the verse to gain more understanding of your responsibility to study God's Word. The words "rightly divides" in the King James version of the Bible actually come from one Greek word which means to make a straight cut, i.e., to dissect (expound) correctly (the divine message).

To dissect means: to cut apart; cut up piece by piece; separate into parts for the purpose of study, examination, and analysis.

To Expound means: to set forth point by point; state in detail; to explain; make clear; interpret; clarify.

Does anyone remember having to dissect an animal in biology class, or was I the only one being traumatized by being forced to do it?

Some had to dissect a frog, while others had a lizard, and still others had a pig!

Bringing back any memories?

Back in my day, I had a frog. I remember opening it up and beginning to sort through the various layers of its internal framework, while the teacher described what we were seeing. Layer by layer, the teacher brought a new understanding to the inner workings of the frog as we pulled out organs, separated muscles, and exposed the veins that made this frog move, and breathe and live its life.

It was pretty gross!

I can't say that it was different than what I'd imagined because up until that point, I had certainly never had any cause to imagine what the inner workings of a frog would look like. I just knew it was quite different from what I had ever seen before. But no matter what I thought about it, or how gross I thought the process was, I *had* to come to the conclusion that those "strange" internal workings must be what made this animal live, and move, jump, and breathe.

The frog had now been dissected, and each portion of its anatomy had been exposed and expounded upon to discover its purpose in the biology of the frog. I had examined that frog both inside and externally, every which way I could—to discover the truth of the frog's existence.

By the same token, when you rightly divide or dissect God's Word, you might discover some aspects that look strange and foreign compared to what you've previously been taught, but you *must* conclude that this is His Word rightly divided—properly cut apart, separated into pieces for the purposes of study, examination, and analysis. And it is only through these strange, properly dissected internal workings that you learn to live and move and have *your* being in Christ. You can then say that you have looked at it and examined it thoroughly from every conceivable perspective, and found it to be correct and understood.

Then we're commanded to hold fast to that truth.

This is *exactly* what we're about to do with the topic of true worship.

We're going to take it apart piece by piece, examining and analyzing those pieces, then setting forth precisely what they mean point by point. I shall state in detail what the Word of God is saying, so you can get an understanding of what true worship is, and why God is seeking it so strongly.

When we complete the process of dissecting and expounding upon this topic, you will see that true worship is first and foremost a condition of the heart. You will see that this condition of the heart will *always* be primary, but it will also *contain* an external position of the body. Finally, you will find that these components are given to God both publicly and privately.

Why do all this? Is it necessary that you get this kind of understanding? Why require such exploration and depth of understanding? Can't you just accept it is as it appears? Can't we all just do that?

These are the kinds of questions I sometimes get at this point in the study.

The answers are, of course, that we do all this—and *must* do all this—because we love Him, and we want to be obedient and give Him what He's looking for.

It's necessary to get a depth of understanding of the topic because you can't give something if you don't understand what it is you are to give. Can you? How can you give God something without understanding what that *something* comprises, that you're to give? You can't—it's impossible!

You need the thorough and complete understanding first.

That's what I hope to accomplish with you as we continue.

That's what you should be seeking during the course of this study.

> *Proverbs 4:7 says, "Wisdom is the principal thing; therefore, get wisdom. And in all your getting, get understanding."*

So, we're going to get an understanding of this topic *through* rightly dividing it.

By the way, that verse says, "Wisdom is the principle thing…"

What do you take from that? What is wisdom? It's spoken of prominently throughout the Bible. The Strong's Concordance has the Hebrew word for wisdom in this verse, coming from a root word that means: to be wise in mind, word, or act.

In Webster's 1828 version of the dictionary, the first definition of wisdom is: the right use or exercise of knowledge; the choice of laudable ends; and of the best means to accomplish them. This is wisdom in act, effect, or practice. In short, this means wisdom is the right and appropriate use or application of knowledge, or that it is knowledge applied properly.

In Proverbs 4:7, wisdom is the principal thing, but to get wisdom, you need knowledge and understanding of a topic. Therefore, they work in concert with each other. You need knowledge and understanding first to properly apply it, which is exactly where wisdom comes in.

Makes sense?

Give some time to considering this, so that you can truly grasp this principle and understand why you should be incorporating the search for knowledge and understanding into every aspect of your life.

Therefore, you should strive to gain a thorough and complete knowledge and understanding of what true worship is, then use wisdom—the proper exercise of that knowledge—to *apply* what you've learned to your life.

CHAPTER THREE

JOHN 4

Our main Scriptural text for this topic of discussion will be based on John 4:23-24.

Before you get there, it can be helpful to read previous portions of the chapter to get the flow of ideas, and what was taking place, thereby framing the context of what is being said in this portion of Scripture.

In John 4:1-4, Jesus was leaving Judea and heading to Galilee, and this journey needed to pass through Samaria. Most knew that the road through Samaria was the shortest route to Galilee, but pious Jews were in the habit of completely avoiding it. At that time, Jewish people didn't like the Samaritans, considering them half-bred Jews who had forsaken the worship of the true God. So, the angst between them had grown to the point where many Jews avoided even walking through what they recognized as Samaritan land.

In John 4:5-9, Jesus arrived at a well in Sychar, the capital of Samaria, at a parcel of land that the ancient Jewish forefather, Jacob, had given to his son Joseph. Jesus was tired as it was almost the sixth hour of the day, or about noon.

John 4:7-19, tells of Jesus speaking with a Samaritan woman, telling her things about her life after she showed up to draw some water. Jesus asked her to draw water for Him as well, because His disciples had gone into the city to buy meat.

Here, it was the first time the woman noticed the difference between Jesus and other Jews. As previously noted, in those days, Jews had no dealings with the Samaritans. For Jesus to even speak to her, that set Him apart from perhaps every other Jew she had ever encountered.

Jesus began to tell her about the living water that only He could provide. She asked Him for some of this living water to drink, so He told her to bring her husband along with her to draw it. She said she had no husband.

Jesus then expounded to her things about her life that, had He been a normal man, He couldn't possibly have known, telling her that she had spoken correctly because she previously had five husbands, and the man she was with now was not her husband.

Let's begin reading there at that point in the exchange: John 4:19 – 22.

> *19 "The woman says unto Him, Sir I perceive you are a prophet.*
>
> *20 Our fathers worshiped in this mountain and you say that in Jerusalem is the place where men ought to worship.*
>
> *21 Jesus said unto her, Woman, believe me, the hour comes, when you shall neither in this mountain, nor at Jerusalem, worship the Father.*
>
> *22 You worship what you know not: we know what we worship: for salvation is of the Jews."*

At that time, their people worshiped either on that mountain (the Samaritans), or in Jerusalem (the Jews). The Samaritans believed that Moses commissioned an altar on Mount Gerizim, the mountain of blessing; this was why they believed that worship on that particular mountain was correct.

And the Jews for centuries had Jerusalem, the city of peace, as their place of communion with God.

These were the main geographical locations for proper worship for both ethnic groups.

People came from miles around and walked for days on end to reach Jerusalem, to offer sacrifices in worship there. But Jesus pointed out to the woman that a time was coming when worship would no longer be focused on *a physical location*. It wouldn't be on a mountain, or in any Temple, or anywhere else that it had taken place in the past. Things were about to change!

At last, we arrive at our Scripture of focus: John 4:23-24:

> *"But the hour cometh and now is, when the true worshipers shall worship the Father in spirit and in truth: for the Father seeketh such to worship Him.*
> *24 God is a Spirit, and they that worship Him must worship Him in spirit and in truth."*

Let's repeat that again. *The hour is coming, and now is, when those that are truly worshiping the Father shall do it in spirit and in truth.* This means no more mountaintops, and no more journeying to a special city to worship!

Jesus never downgraded the importance of worship; He was merely destroying the sacredly held geographical locations and the outward rites and ceremonies that had accompanied the people's worship.

What Jesus was initiating was a worship in the *hearts* of man, the way God always desired worship to be.

Since Jesus placed emphasis on the kind of worship that was beginning in His day and extending to the present, it is vitally important that we understand exactly what it is, and precisely how we are to give it to the Father. This is something we will focus on throughout this book.

CHAPTER FOUR

THE MEANING OF 'MUST'

Let's go back and look once again at our main verse of study, John 4:23–24:

> *"But the hour cometh and now is, when the true worshipers shall worship the Father in spirit and in truth: for the Father seeketh such to worship Him. God is a Spirit, and they that worship him <u>must</u> worship Him in spirit and in truth."* (Emphasis/underlining by the author.)

Websters 1828 Dictionary says, "Must" means: to be obliged; to be necessitated. It expresses both physical and moral necessity. Without any doubt or get-outs, that means it is mandatory.

Let me be clear and understood; God is not giving a little suggestion here! It's something He *requires* of each of you!

It's an obligation you take upon yourself right here and now, both as a *physical and moral necessity*.

Therefore, by definition, when you discover what it is to worship God in spirit and in truth, no matter what it looks like, no matter what it sounds like, no matter what your feelings may be telling you concerning this topic, it's *mandatory* that you perform it.

You *must*.

This means you have a physical and moral obligation to put what you've learned into practice, and to do this right away. No ifs, ands, or buts. No further interpretations, subjectivity, delays, half-measures, or excuses.

You *must*.

A complimentary Scripture states:

> *"For unto whom much is given, of him shall much be required..." Lk. 12:48.*

The main idea behind this verse is that you are held responsible for that with which you have been entrusted.

Each one of you has been blessed with an array of talents, gifts, wealth, knowledge, time, and the like, and it is expected that you will use what you have been given to glorify God—and that you shall use all of it, all of the time, for Him. Faithful stewardship *requires* that you manage what you've been given wisely, which as you've seen, is the proper application of the knowledge and understanding that you've received.

God says once you are given truth, *you are held responsible.*

Once you learn the truth of true worship, you *must*, and it's mandatory, that you apply that truth to your life. Don't just know it—use it.

CHAPTER FIVE

'SEEKETH/SEEKS'

> *"But the hour cometh and now is, when the true worshipers shall worship the Father in spirit and in truth: for the Father <u>seeketh</u> such to worship Him. God is a Spirit, and they that worship Him must worship Him in spirit and in truth."*
>
> *- KJV, John 4:23-24*

The next word I want you to look at in our verse is 'seeketh'. Some translations prefer the more common usage, 'seeks'. "Seeketh/Seeks", according to Strong's Concordance online, 2212, Greek; *zeteo* means: 1) to look for, to seek, to inquire after or about, to seek [in order to find out] by thinking, meditating, reasoning, to enquire into, to seek after, seek for, aim at, strive after, endeavoring to find, to actively pursue finding out, to bend one's efforts toward trying to find. 2) to seek—i.e. require, demand, to crave, demand something from someone.

Look at those definitions again. Read them slowly.

Remember, this is God we're talking about. The same God of the universe who created all things, yet humiliated Himself by coming to earth and suffering the most horrifying death that the mind of man has ever conceived, so that you and I could be a part of His family and rule with Him forever.

That God is looking for, seeking, inquiring about, actively pursuing, and bending His efforts toward trying to find something….. *from you.*

That in itself is mindboggling, don't you agree? *God* wants something from *you?*

He's God! He's so big and powerful; how could tiny little insignificant man—insignificant *you or me*—possibly possess *anything* that God wants?

But there it is, in black and white. God is *seeking* something. From you.

The realization truly hit home when I began to personalize it.

Now, it became: *God* is seeking, endeavoring to find, and desiring something from *me*.

Think about this, read it, and speak it aloud.

'*God* is seeking, endeavoring to find, and desiring something from *me*'.

Everyone reading these pages should realize that God is desiring something from *you*. And it's something you have the ability to give, and something each of you *must* give.

In the definition and use of the word 'zeteo' or 'seeks', what's being sought after is so earnestly desired that it actually takes on the far stronger connotation of something being *craved* and *demanded* by another.

God desires your worship. That's true.

But there's also coming a time when God will *demand it* from every creature under heaven.

> *Philippians 2:10-11 states:" that at the name of Jesus every knee should bow, of those in heaven, and of those on earth, and of those under the earth,* [11] *and that every tongue should confess that Jesus Christ is Lord, to the glory of God the Father".*

This bowing of the knee and confessing with their tongues is being forced. They are being *compelled* to comply, whether they like to or not.

Of course, those of you who know and love Him will do it willingly, and without reservation, since you naturally and wholeheartedly desire to please Him. But those of you who have refused to submit to God's Will in that day, will be *compelled* to surrender and acknowledge Him as the universe's supreme authority!

You have the opportunity to fully surrender to Him *right now*; you can already give Him what He's been desiring and have Him respond to you lovingly.

So, why wait, and why delay?

You cannot keep giving God less than the best that you have. You cannot keep giving Him something different than what He's seeking and longing for, yet constantly expect Him to respond in the ways that you want or have read within the pages of Scripture. Can you?

This is a poor example, but I'll give it anyway.

A friend of mine had an anniversary coming up and he knew that his wife was longing for something special. He didn't think she had anything in particular in mind, but as we talked, I told him that she probably just wanted to know that he was thinking about her.

Every woman wants to feel special. And as we spoke more, he felt his wife probably longed to rekindle certain emotions that over the years seem to have waned between them.

We spoke of several options, from inexpensive to mildly expensive, that would seem to fit their circumstance. One was as simple as sending her a bouquet of flowers while she was at work, and for the rest of the day, she would feel like a princess! We envisioned colleagues stopping by her desk, telling her how beautiful her flowers were, and how lucky she was to have a man sensitive enough to send them.

Another was a weekend for two at a nice hotel, or a romantic bed-and-breakfast getaway.

I was pretty confident we had come up with some very nice suggestions that would send the message that he was not only thinking of her, but thinking of her in the very same way he had done when they'd first met and got married. I was sure he had taken away from our lengthy discussion plenty of amazing, heartwarming ideas for how to spoil his wonderful wife on her special day, and I really looked forward to hearing what treat he had given her and how she had received it. It was nice, too, to know I had been able to play a small part.

Well, long story short, he bought her a vacuum sweeper.

Yep, he *really* did.

I couldn't believe it!

He actually thought he was doing a good thing because it was an expensive vacuum, and their old one had broken down several times, making her chores doubly tiresome. So, in his mind, he was buying something both expensive *and* practical, so she should really love it! Right?

As you can maybe imagine, his gift didn't go over too well.

Isn't this exactly how we treat God?

We give Him whatever *we* want to give Him, and we never stop to consider whether what we're giving is what He actually wants and craves. Then we settle into the perspective that we are doing what's required because we perform the weekly church attendance and tithing routine. But He doesn't desire our attendance or our tithes, He wants our hearts! But our hearts are far from Him.

Is this you?

Like my friend's situation with his wife, are you taking the easy route and giving the practical gift which shows no underlying passion, while dismissing the heartfelt gift God is truly desiring?

God has always been, and always will be longing for the totality of your heart. Anything less is doing Him a *great* disservice.

'SEEKETH/SEEKS'

A wise friend of mine coined a phrase that I've been using for years now because it's absolutely true, and applicable in the vast majority of spiritual perspectives.

"The heart is the one thing God wants, but it's the one thing He *will not take*. It must be given." M. Heiman

Anything, and everything else you do for God or give Him, must be tempered through *this* lens.

If your heart is not in it, He doesn't want it.

Period.

Once you understand that, the totality of the concept of true worship becomes much easier to comprehend and apply to your life.

God has been asking for us to worship Him truly. Instead, this is what happens. We go to church, sing a few obligatory songs, listen to another dispassionate message, and then go home to live life exactly how *we* want to live it, without God, until we come back to church to do it all again just as dispassionately—and sometimes, even disingenuously—the next Sunday.

Then we get angry because we don't see or experience the power of God in our church's or in our personal lives. Well, should that really be any surprise?

He's asking for—craving and seeking—our hearts, and yet some people are still giving Him jaded, thoughtless apathy. That's exactly the *opposite* of what He wants!

That's the vacuum sweeper!

If I were Him, I would be seriously upset with those who do this.

Worship has nothing to do with singing. It has nothing to do with going to church every Sunday morning, or with preaching or teaching either. In case you're wondering, it has nothing to do with anything that you religiously *perform routinely and habitually* in this life! Remember, Jesus willfully destroyed those rites and ceremonies, and those performances that you carry out to make *your* type of worship, the type of worship that's easiest to do and that happens to fit your life the best.

He brought in a worship which was—and is, and always will be—about an activity of the heart!

It can *contain* singing, preaching, and teaching, and most other things you do in life, bu*t only* when your heart is in the proper condition. The heartfelt part of this is the only part that matters! The heart and the passion, and the deep-felt devotion, are what He seeks, not the rites and the habits, and the *look at me going to church* that people so often conduct, simply so that you're seen to be doing the right thing—or the supposed good thing.

I hope that makes sense.

Anyway, back to my friend and his situation with his wife and the vacuum sweeper.

It took me quite a long time to convince him of the error in his thought process concerning his wife, but eventually, he got it. (Better late than never, as the saying goes).

From then on, he started throwing practicality out the window, and began giving her small gifts simply because he loved her, and because he wanted to see that big, beautiful smile on her face again.

And *oh my!* She responded in the most gratifying way! Now she feels loved, and he feels appreciated, and they both feel like their marriage has been infused with a new level of caring.

So, what do you think would happen if, instead of giving God what *you* feel like giving Him, you started loving Him in the way *He desires* for you to love Him?

Do you think He would respond to you differently if you started giving Him the one thing that He's seeking, and longing for? Do you think He would come into your circumstance and reveal Himself through incredible spiritual manifestations like those spoken of in Scripture? Do you think these efforts to give God what He craves and yearns for—in place of what's easiest or most convenient to give—would bring Him closer to you in your daily life? Of course they will! Try it and see.

You each have an opportunity *right now* to give God exactly what He's looking for.

When you do, that's when things will start to get amazing for you.

When He finds what He's been looking for, seeking, actively bending His efforts toward trying to find, He comes into that life, and he will commune with you in a more intimate way than you've ever known previously. And you'll get to bask in His presence as He envelops you in His love.

It is really all very simple, far simpler than you would imagine it to be. Why do people have to make what God wants sound so complicated or unreachable?

All He's looking for is for you to worship Him in the only way that He truly desires.

That is all He is asking for from each of us.

This teaching has gone around the world, and yet so many reasons are given for why people still won't give God the exact kind of worship that He's looking for.

After finding out what is involved, some have said, "I don't believe it takes all that." Or "God wouldn't require me to do that!"

Others refuse to believe the rightly divided and clearly expounded Word of God in this area, saying, "Although I can't refute it, I just refuse to believe it."

But the majority of those who refuse to apply their acquired knowledge on true worship, simply know that this type of worship will make them feel uncomfortable. They don't protest it, or refute it, but they simply leave it alone and do nothing about it, choosing instead to stay with the comfortable, familiar, 'normal' kind of worship services they've become accustomed to.

Could that be you?

Regardless of the reasons, each of you must come to your own conclusions concerning one question; once you discover and gain an understanding concerning what God is looking for, will you give Him that which He desires from you?

The all-powerful God of the universe is looking for, seeking, inquiring about, actively pursuing, and bending His efforts toward trying to find something *from you*.

Will you give it to Him, or will you continue to give Him what *you want* to give Him, and then praise yourself for being so generous?

You need to become a doer of the Word and not a hearer only, as Scripture says, then use wisdom to properly apply the knowledge gained to your life.

CHAPTER SIX

'TRUE'

> *"But the hour cometh and now is, when the <u>true</u> worshipers shall worship the Father in spirit and in <u>truth</u>: for the Father seeketh such to worship Him. God is a Spirit, they that worship Him must worship Him in spirit and in <u>truth</u>."* (Emphasis/ underlining by the author).
>
> *- John 4:23-24*

To begin rightly dividing this verse, let's look at the word "True/ truth", and what it means in Greek.

In Strong's Concordance, number 228 is the word 'alethinos' (pronounced al-lay-thee-nos) which means truthful or true. Thayer's Greek Lexicon adds: 'Without error. What is true and correct in any matter under consideration. As the case is, according to fact'.

What would be true under *any* circumstance, no matter where you go in the world, or what you're experiencing?

God's Word! It *never* changes and is always truthful and true.

No matter the culture, circumstances, or your experiences, the Word of God stands as the only measure of unchanging truth in this life. You can stand on it through the winds of change in *your* life. It never changes because your God never changes.

> *Malachi 3:6 says: "For I am the Lord, I change not."*
>
> *Hebrews 13:8 states that: "Jesus Christ the same yesterday, and today, and forever."*
>
> *And John 1:14 says: "the Word became flesh and dwelt among us, and we beheld his glory as of the only begotten of the Father."*

Jesus is the Word that became flesh and lived among us. And He is the same yesterday, today and forever. He doesn't change, and He is the Word; therefore, the Word never changes. It is *that* which provides stability in your life throughout any circumstances you may go through.

So, the Word of God is truth, and remains unchanged through any circumstances in your life.

This is what is meant by the word 'truth' in our Scripture. You are to worship God in spirit and in truth, or in the unchanging perfection of the Word of God.

It is to place such esteem upon the living Word of God that *everything* else in life is seen through the perspective of your faith and your trust in this unchanging and perfect truth.

But wait! There's more!

Roget's Thesaurus is a book in which many synonyms of a word can be found. (Synonyms are words with the same meaning). Some of Roget's synonyms for the word *true* are faithful, constant, loyal, sincere, correct, accurate, steadfast, and undeviating. So, true means accurate and consistent, but also loyal and steadfast.

These are just *some* of the adjectives used to describe the word true, and therefore, according to our Bible verse, showing what a *true* worshiper is. I won't labor the point and discuss all of the synonyms here, but just enough for you to gain more understanding of this critical word in this topic.

From Websters 1828 dictionary, the word constant means: fixed; firm; opposed to fluid. Fixed; not varied; unchanged; permanent; immutable. Firm in mind, purpose, affection, or principle; unshaken; unmoved.

In other words, constant means fixed, unchanging, not varied but the same—all the time.

How about the definition of the word *accurate?* It means in exact conformity to truth, or to a standard or rule, or to a model, free from failure, error, or defect.

What does undeviating mean? Not deviating; not departing from the way, or from a rule, principle, or purpose; steady; regular; as an undeviating course of virtue. Not erring; not wandering; not crooked.

For many of you, some of these words probably seem to be conveying the same idea.

Before I started studying true worship, I also thought accuracy and precision were the same thing. But when studying the different definitions, I began to see a uniqueness in each of the words. After speaking with a close friend who has worked as an engineer in the U.S. Government's Naval Nuclear Propulsion Program for many years, and who consistently uses some of these terms in a real-world engineering context, my understanding of these two words became more complete.

As our definition makes clear, accuracy is how close the measurements are to the true value, or to a standard.

Precision means something executed or successively repeated within closely specified limits.

The difference is that precision is how the process is successively repeated, meaning those closely specified limits are determined by the proximity of the measurements to *each other*. It's repeating a process and successfully having all the measurements within an exceedingly small, specified limit of one another.

See the difference?

In other words, you can have a group of people or instruments with similar answers that are successively repeated and precise, but they are all still incorrect. That is precision. The precision group, although almost exactly the same in measurement and value, have totally missed the mark. Their exactness is measured solely by how close they are to *each other*.

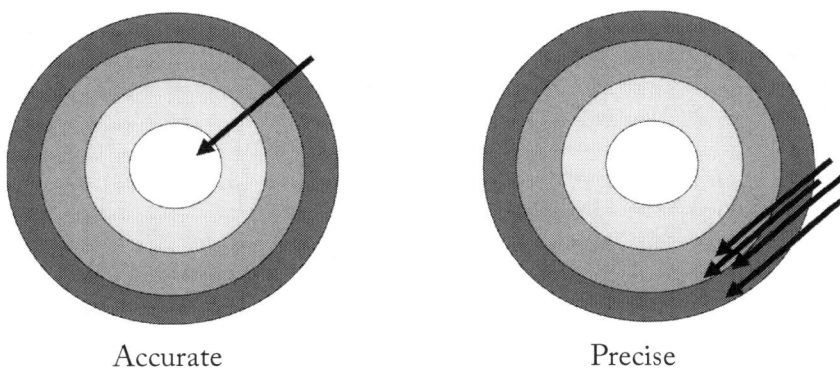

Accurate   Precise

This is why standards are used throughout the scientific and engineering communities. Standards tell you what the *true* answer is. There *has* to be a standard—a value that is known and accepted—to gauge whether or not procedures and instruments are not only precise and consistently get answers close to each other, but are *also* accurate or in perfect accord with that standard.

So, what is the application for accuracy and precision in our current study of true worship, or even in our daily Christian walk of life? One application is that the majority of churches have been practicing worship in the same manner for many years. Their 'worship' services have all come to look almost exactly alike.

Sure enough, they may be precise, which shows how close in proximity they are with *each other*, meaning they are all remarkably similar. But is the 'worship' according to the standard?

As I continue to unpack what true worship is, you will see that much of what has been taking place in our churches may not be worship at all, but a consistent and reliable missing of the mark.

Many church services don't have the accuracy because their 'worship' is not in accordance with the standard of Scripture. The Bible is your ultimate standard against which you should measure yourself. It tells you what the true answers are. So, as you proceed with learning what true worship is, you need to keep in mind that your personal goal, and *indeed, the goal of this book*, is to arm the Church with understanding in this matter, so you can be—individually and corporately—accurate *and* precise! Then *every* time, the Church will be worshiping according to the standard of Scripture, *and* consistently hitting the bullseye!

Makes sense?

Then let's go back to the original verse and put this all together.

> *"But the hour cometh, and now is, when the true worshipers shall worship the Father in spirit and truth: for the Father seeks such to worship Him. (24) God is Spirit, and they that worship Him must worship Him in spirit and in truth."*
>
> *- John 4:23-24*

So, a true worshiper is one who worships faithfully and constantly, which is all the time. The worship they render to God is accurate, which means in exact accordance with truth or to the standard of God's Word. And they are undeviating in their worship, so that once the correct and accurate path is found, they don't ever stray from it.

As each one of you reads through the definitions defining the characteristics of the word true, you'll begin to see that perhaps you've been falling short of being true to God, and by extension, you've been untrue to the worship that's been due to Him. But a constant, faithful, accurate and undeviating worshiper is who God is seeking. This is what it means to be true.

Here's another bit of information that stunned me when I first learned about it.

I realized that within every one of the definitions that I had gleaned, there was a negative side that had to be given consideration as well. I also realized that, unfortunately at the time, I was a part of this latter category.

I wasn't being true.

If a constant worshiper is one who worships all the time, then worshiping constantly is what God is seeking. The implication is that God is *not* seeking, and He does *not* desire, one who only gives Him a *part-time* worship.

If part of being true also means to be accurate, or that which is according to an exact standard or manner, then this implies that there is a worship that is *inaccurate,* that God is *not* seeking.

And lastly, if there is an undeviating worship God desires and toward which He is bending His efforts trying to find, then there is a worship that deviates from the correct path—which God has no desire for, nor does He take pleasure in it.

For many, if you're honest with yourselves, you would admit that maybe you aren't as constant as you need to be. Or maybe you'd see how you've deviated from time to time from the worship that you knew only belonged to God.

Others of you simply never knew what was expected of you because you didn't understand what true worship was all about. We're going to rectify this as we move along, so that each of you can act on the new knowledge you will gain and give God what He's been looking for—both accurately and consistently.

Let's put your new understanding into our Scripture verse.

> *But the hour cometh, and now is, when the*
> *true (the faithful, constant – all the time, accurate –*

correct, and undeviating – never moving from the proper path) worshippers shall worship the Father in spirit and in truth: for the Father seeketh (is looking for, desiring, bending His efforts towards trying to find) such to worship Him. (Vs 24): God is a Spirit; and they that worship Him must (it's mandatory) worship Him in spirit and in truth (the only thing that is always accurate and undeviating wherever you are, and in whatever circumstances you find yourself – the Word of God).

- John 4:23-24

CHAPTER SEVEN

WHAT IS A WORSHIPER?

Strong's Concordance (4353), Worshiper; Greek - proskunetes, (praws-koon-net-is); an adorer.

The first thing you see is that a worshiper is an adorer. The words are synonymous.

From the Websters Dictionary, the definition of the term 'adoration' is to love with the deepest of affections. It consists in an external homage, accompanied with the highest reverence, and the paying of honors to a divine being. It is great love, devotion, and respect.

Everything associated with this type of worship has the strongest adjectives that can possibly be used in the English language to describe it. It's not just respect, it's the *greatest* respect you can give. It's not just honor, but the *highest* honor. It is not simply a casual type of love, but to love with your *strongest* affections, and with the utmost (deepest) portions of your being.

The word *adore,* from adoration, means to worship as divine, to love greatly, honor highly, idolize, revere.

If you look at the word adore, it comes from two Latin words, 'ad' and 'orare'. Together, they mean *to speak* or *to voice*. There's an oral element that comes with adoration or adoring someone, a declaration.

Have you ever been in love before?

The stronger the feelings of love grow, the more it begins to overwhelm the heart until you just can't help but tell your friends and family about this new love that you found—in a voicing, a declaration of love. Most times, you can't even help it. You want to spend time with them, learning all about who they are, their likes and dislikes, their family, etc. This overwhelming feeling within you comes out in how you think, and the things you do. You don't even have to try, as it simply bubbles up out of you. That's true love, adoration.

We are to learn to love God that way, where it just bubbles up out of you and you can't help but think about Him, talk about Him, and be thrilled to be in His presence again.

Scripture says:

> *"From the abundance of the heart, the mouth speaks."*

This means that whatever is abundant and overflowing within your heart will eventually come out of your mouth. This is so true in every area of life, but none more so than in the area of adoration.

This love so overwhelms you that you can't help but tell the world about it.

Therefore, a worshiper is an adorer *so* in love with God that they can't help but orally declare the great love they have for Him at every possible opportunity.

Please understand this. Adoration is the highest and most intimate form of what we call worship. It can make *your* worship 'true' because your heart is involved and invested. Think about it. If you truly adore God with all of your heart, you will want to *constantly* be in His presence. You will know that you are *accurately* and *faithfully* giving Him what He desires, which gives you great pleasure as He comes into your immediate presence and you undeviatingly fall down and pour out your heart to Him in adoration.

This, the inclusion, and activity of the heart, is why a true worshiper is not *primarily* about singing, going to church, or performing any outward rituals.

It is first and foremost about forming and nurturing an internal relationship with God. It's about intimacy. *Everything* external, any physical position or action you discuss, flows outward from that intimate internal relationship. The resulting intimacy acquired through this adoration of God results in changes in every part of the Christian's life. It is the difference between knowing *about* God and knowing God.

The Theology of Adoration

> *"If we are only allowed one expression in our lives, it must be the adoration of God. Any other focus of our lives or anything else added to that is idolatry.*
>
> *"The best obedience of my hands dares not appear before thy throne."*

WHAT IS A WORSHIPER?

> *"To whatever degree we focus on obedience, we take that focus off of adoration for the Lord, and in doing so we are asking the Lord to share His throne with our works."*
>
> – Poet, Isaac Watts

These are powerful statements.

But are they true?

It appears to be the truth if you look at the end result of focusing upon obedience. That focus centers your thoughts and actions around performance, rather than allowing you to cultivate the heart conditions of love and gratitude necessary for adoring God.

I honestly believe we, in the Christian community, start out sincerely attempting to reconcile the love we have for God, with keeping His commands. We never realize that in attempting this reconciliation, we're actually walking a tightrope between two powerful enemies called the flesh and the spirit.

And since most Christians have never learned about the power of their fleshly nature and how to push it aside and ignore it, we end up leaning toward the tendency to *do* more for God instead of engaging in the more spiritual activity of *adoring* God with our hearts.

The bottom line in understanding adoration is knowing that if you genuinely want to obey God, then you need to try to forget about all the do's and don'ts, retraining your focus upon spending the time to come before Him in adoration. It's more about a *relationship* with God than a list of things you need to accomplish in order to appease Him. Let go of all of your striving to *do*, and just *be*.

In John 14:15, Jesus makes a powerful statement. He says:

"If you love me, keep my commandments".

Couple that with 1 John 2:3-4, which says,

> *"And hereby do we know that we know Him, if we keep His commandments. (4) He that professes to know Him, and does not keep His commandments, is a liar and the truth is not in him."*

Here, you have two important verses of Scripture stating that if you love Jesus, you'll keep His commandments, and if you don't keep His commandments, you don't know Him, and the truth is not in you. Therefore, it is *vitally* important that you learn what He's referring to. What are the commandments He's given you to keep, so you can begin to love and honor Him through them?

Before we go any further, I have to make sure that we are on the same page with our understanding of a few things. Again, I pray this isn't too harsh for some of you to hear, but unfortunately, it's the truth.

For the most part, Christians don't worship a triune God of Father, Son, and Holy Spirit. Instead, they worship a four-headed deity consisting of Father, Son, Holy Spirit, and their works or obedience.

Unfortunately, this is where I was for most of my life too, so I understand how easy it is for what I *do* for God to creep up in importance alongside my *relationship* with Him.

Ultimately, this results in the *works* stemming from our obedience—even though coming from a heart longing to *do* for God—being elevated and worshiped *with* God.

When Jesus says, "If you love me, keep my commandments", we have a tendency to think, "OK, Lord, I'm going to keep a commandment to prove that I love You."

In other words, you're going to attempt to *do* something, or you're going to be obedient in this area or that, to prove that you love. Many times, it's just easier for us to condense all that we read in Scripture down to a list of do's and don'ts so we can perform the proper ritual or religious action that proves that we love God.

Unfortunately, this is a slippery slope.

Can you see how easy it is to fall into that mode of thinking? We do it all the time.

This is how many churches have become works-based entities that move through this life without the cloud of God's presence going before them. They never take the time to realize that actually, they've left Him far behind, choosing instead to cling to performance-centered traditions, and/or works-based religious activities to appease Him. But that's *not* what Jesus was saying. Not at all!

If you look at the totality of Jesus' ministry, you realize that His words were always directed at the *hearts* of His listeners. At one point, He even spoke of a false worship within this context, saying:

> *"With their lips they worship me, but their hearts are far from me."*

Anyone can talk a good game, can't they? But is your heart fully involved and invested in the activity? Jesus was always focused upon the heart.

Let's be clear about this and leave no room for misunderstanding.

You can 'do' any actions consistently and routinely or habitually, and you can even do these actions flawlessly, too—but in no way do these works and performances show you love God.

Remember this, works *follow* faith, but faith does not necessarily follow works.

Once a belief is in the heart, works will be done outwardly to verify what's inside. The inside is the beginning, and the core. Conversely, faith won't necessarily always follow works. In other words, just because I see someone feeding the hungry, which is a good, admirable, and perhaps even a pious religious activity, it does not necessarily follow that those performing it are dedicated Christians in the faith. It does not necessarily mean they are pious.

It may mean—for example—that they do it to draw attention and admiration to themselves. Is that pious?

You who are true lovers of Christ and trusting in Him for your salvation, should have a natural tendency to move toward compassion, so that when you see a person in need, you naturally move to help them. You do this with no thought whatsoever of who is watching, of who is standing by to praise or admire you, or of what you might get back from it. The outward work of helping others should naturally flow from your love of and belief in the compassionate Christ. Your outward work should come from the heart that drives you.

Therefore, when Jesus says, *"If you love me, keep my commandments"*, He wasn't saying do this or do that to prove your love. He was saying that *if* your focus is set on loving me, you *will* keep my commandments. He was saying it would occur naturally, by default. The outpouring of love for Me will so transform you, so that you won't have to *try* to be obedient; it will simply begin to flow from you, without you even noticing it.

If you find it difficult to grasp the concept of outward works needing to flow naturally from the inner heart, think of a simple comparison. Does it follow that a parent is bestowing their deepest, purest love upon a child when they shower the child with gifts or buy them the latest gadgets and fashions, or take them away on fancy vacations that will make the child the envy of all their friends? No, it absolutely doesn't. Of course, we all know that the mother who loves her child with all of her heart may well buy the child such things and wish to spoil them—and that this will then be a natural follow-up to adoring the child.

But the reverse is not always true, that bestowing gifts and taking a child here and there, and showering them with expenditure *means* love and adoration.

How many times do you hear full-grown adults speak of their upbringings in which they were showered with material possessions and treats—and yet never felt loved? They were never hugged, or kissed, and never praised or told they had done well when they came last in the running race at school.

You see the difference?

Here, the doing, the giving, the *performance* also is no measure whatsoever of the extent of adoration in the heart. Indeed, in some cases, the doing and the performing are outward shows—for the sake of going through the motions and to be seen to do the 'right' things. To some degree, they could also be a means to assuage the guilt of not delivering the heartfelt love that the child craves and deserves.

So, it is the same when you give to God. The giving and the outer shows, the regular acts that you perform at church are not at all what He desires, seeks, or craves. These are the routine and habitual doings that really show nothing at all, *unless* driven by and naturally emerging from the adoration of the heart, which must be at the center of everything you should be doing to show Him your love.

The outer giving in itself will not lead to feeling this necessary inner, heartfelt adoration.

Outer giving may even be a cover-up for the inability to feel adoration or for the lack of effort, energy and thought about the best way to show your love for, and devotion to, God.

If nothing else, remember this; giving to God properly begins only with the heart, and if this should be lacking, then the giving, and the outward demonstrations of *doing*, all count for nothing.

Let's look at a biblical principle.

> *Luke 6:45: "From the abundance of the heart, the mouth speaks."*

This is saying that whatever is overflowing in your heart will eventually come out of your mouth, no matter whether you intend it to or not. You can't help it. It flows out of your mouth naturally just like we proclaimed the love for a romantic partner to our friends and family, as I mentioned earlier.

James 2:20 says, "Faith without works is dead".

This famous Scripture tells you that when you have faith, belief, and confidence, and when you are persuaded and trust in God, when you rely upon Him and upon His Word, (all these constituting the definitions of faith) and when all this resides within your heart—works or actions *must* naturally follow from it. He's saying the same thing over and over in Scripture, that what's inside *has* to come out.

There's no fighting it.

That's why Jesus said, if you look on a woman with lust in your heart, you've already committed adultery. And if you hate your brother, you've already committed murder. Because what's inside is going to come out. What's overflowing within your heart is coming out, whether in your words or in your actions, or both.

This principle is based upon all of these Scriptures, and it shows that whatever is in your heart, good or bad, will simply begin to flow outwardly from you. You don't have to think about doing it, plan it or structure it, or cultivate the practice of it—since it will ooze out of every pore of your being without you even noticing or trying.

This concept is of utmost importance, therefore, I pray it makes sense to you.

If you feel at all unsure, please stop reading further for now, revisiting all the parts you have just read until you are sure you understand.

Listen, obedience is important! I don't want to understate that.

But if you can begin to center your heart and mind upon the Lord, His goodness, and all He's done for you, you will unconsciously cease worrying about your obedience—because that focus and energy will *already be where it belongs,* on cultivating a sincere and heartfelt love for God's presence.

From that, you'll be fully acceptable in the eyes of God, and as a secondary effect of that focus, you will be more obedient without even thinking about it.

Obedience flows from love, which emerges from the heart, sitting at the core of everything.

This is the proper sequence of importance that you should place on love and obedience.

Love always comes first because it is from the heart!

Obedience by itself doesn't have to have a heart component. You can do all the right things and still maintain the wrong motives, and God will *not* be pleased with you. Remember, many of the Pharisees showed a perfect obedience to the letter of God's Law, yet never recognized Him—though God was standing right there in front of them in Jesus! Their hearts weren't right, that's why.

Cultivate your heart toward God, and obedience will fall in line as a result.

Back to Jesus' statement.

> *John 14:15 says, "If you love me, keep my commandments".*

Which commandments specifically did Jesus tell us to keep?

> *Matthew 22:36-40 reads: "Master, which is the great commandment in the law? (37) Jesus said unto him, "Thou shalt love the Lord thy God with all thy heart, and all thy soul, and all thy mind. (38) This is the first and great commandment (39) And the second is like unto it, Thou shalt love thy neighbor as thyself (40) On these two commandments hang all the law and the prophets."*

Look at verse 40 again. On these two commandments, hang *all* the law and the prophets, so if you simply do these two commandments, you'll be fulfilling all the law and the prophets.

That's crazy, isn't it?

Well, let's consider what *is* the law and the prophets.

The first five books of the Bible are called the Pentateuch, or the Torah, or the Law of Moses. And the prophets are basically the remainder of the Old Testament. Of course, there are a couple of books that may not easily fit into those categories, like Psalms and Proverbs etc., but you get the idea. Most of the Old Testament is fulfilled in these two commandments that Jesus is telling you to do.

And it makes sense when you really think about it. Think about each of the Ten Commandments when you read this. If you love your neighbor as yourself, you definitely won't want to kill them, covet, or desire what they have, steal their material goods, or commit adultery with their spouse!

And once you determine how you are to love God with all your heart, soul, mind, and strength, you'll find that you won't place other gods before Him or provoke Him to jealousy. It all works!

Let's examine now what loving God with all your heart, soul and mind really means.

What does it look like?

These are important questions if you are to fulfill what God wants from you. Too many of us gloss over these verses and never come to any conclusion on what it is Jesus is saying. But how will you give Him something if you are clueless about what it is, or what it even looks like? You can't!

What do people tend to focus on in this passage of Scripture?

I'll give you a hint.

Since most people don't have understanding of the first part of the passage, '…loving God with all our heart and soul and mind,' they focus on the part that makes sense to them, the easy part: '…Love thy neighbor as thyself.'

Many a Christian has concluded that the *way* they love the Lord with all their heart and all their soul, and all their mind, is by loving their neighbor as they love themselves.

Unfortunately, this is inconsistent with the rest of Scripture.

Helping an elderly or disabled person across the street is actually a great example of loving your neighbor as yourself, but this outward action doesn't have to contain your heart. Therefore, this action doesn't come close to showing God that you love *Him* with all your heart and soul and mind.

Hopefully, we'll rehash this subject a little later, but for now, the one thing you need to realize is that God is only after your heart. This is so important to remember that I'll probably mention it several more times.

"The heart is the one thing God wants, but it's the one thing He *will not* take. It has to be given." M. Heiman

This is the crux of adoration.

To love God with all your heart and soul and mind is to love Him with every part of your being! It's placing every faculty at your disposal down at His feet in submission to the God of the universe. It's adoring Him. A lover of God in this all-inclusive manner is an adorer of God. And an adorer of God is a worshiper of God.

> *Matthew 22:37, "Jesus said unto him, Thou shalt love the Lord thy God with all thy heart, and all thy soul, and all thy mind."*

Becoming a true worshiper, adorer, and lover of God is how you fulfill that commandment. And true worship is what loving God in this manner looks like.

Why Should I Adore God?

Let me answer this question first for myself.

I adore God because I want to truly *know* Him. I don't seek Him because I have a need and want to receive from Him. I don't want *stuff*, I want Him. I want closeness. I want intimacy!

When I think about gaining intimacy with God, I can't help but think about the apostle John. You read about John in the Bible and he was always reclining on Jesus' bosom, wasn't he? He would never leave Jesus's side, and so the revelation he received was special because he said things in his gospel that were not recorded anywhere else in Scripture. He came to know secrets that the rest of the disciples, although they were close to Jesus, *never* knew. And it was only because of his intimacy with Christ.

So herein are revealed two of the many reasons why you should adore God.

Adoring God leads you to intimacy with Him. And intimacy with God is a reward greater than anything else you can imagine. The greatest blessing in the universe is that God is with you, and if you only studied to know exactly what that entailed, your life would immediately change.

It doesn't stop there!

Just like the apostle John, your intimacy with Christ brings you into a place where you are able to receive revelation knowledge that others, who may not have as intimate of a relationship with Christ, aren't able to receive.

In John's gospel, Jesus spoke at a table full of His disciples, stating,

> *"The next person that dips in the sop will be the one who betrays me."*

Do you think they *all* heard that? Of course not! If they'd all heard it, nobody would have moved a muscle!

John was the only one close enough to hear, and so he lay reclined with his head on Jesus' chest. He knew when Jesus sighed heavily, when His heartbeat changed from a regular rhythm to a faster one, when Jesus was uncomfortable and had to adjust His position. He knew intimate things that the others *couldn't imagine* knowing.

Think about that for a moment.

Only John received revelatory knowledge of who would betray Jesus.

None of the others had a clue! And it only came because of his intimacy, his closeness with Christ. And lest anyone misunderstand, this is *not* about anyone trying to be better than someone else. You will never acquire the intimacy desired if your heart is based on competition. This is about *knowing* God, and the by-products or benefits of that closer relationship.

Everything we have discussed so far is centered in the heart. Therefore, this is loving God *so* much, that all you long to do is to hear His heartbeat, to know when He sighs heavily, or when something inside of Him becomes agitated. That's the intimacy you should long for, coming out of a desire for Him and Him alone.

Adoring, or loving God with all your heart, and all your soul, and all your mind, and all your strength, leads to intimacy with Him—and intimacy brings all the riches of His presence. I touched only on revelation knowledge, but so many more benefits exist that I couldn't possibly list them all.

> *Jesus said in John 15:10, "If you keep my commandments, you shall abide in my love…"*

What a fantastic promise from God, and another great reason to adore Him. This Scripture describes a way that you can abide, which means to live, dwell, or remain *forever* in His love! We already know that God loved *us* so much that he sent His only Son into the world to die, so that a way could be made for us to have a relationship with Him again. Yes, he loves you *that* much! And *that's* the love you can abide in, live in, and dwell in forever.

Another reason to adore God is that you belong to Him. When you study the topic of redemption, you see that Jesus came into the world and paid the most precious price in the universe for you. He paid with His own blood, with His own life! He then took you out of the marketplace of sin and freed you from the bondage that held you.

Now this portion of redemption is so incredible that many of us never looked into it any further. But Jesus didn't stop there; He didn't just free us from the bondage of sin. He then made us slaves unto Himself.

You no longer belong to yourself. You were bought with a price and belong to Him; Jesus paid the price for you, and you are no longer your own. It's a shift each of us has to make in our minds if we hope to make the jump from self-centeredness to Christ-centeredness.

Many times, in Christian literature or theology, or as you listen in church to pastors or theologians, you hear them say, "You've got to find time in your day for God", or "You've all got to find a way to carve out time to spend with God". Although I understand the sentiments that they are trying to express, I can't help but think it's coming from the wrong perspective. That perspective says everything is yours, and you have to *find* time for the Lord. The time in your day is *yours*, the money you make is *yours*, the talents you have belong to *you*, etc. And your teachers and leaders speak this way because that's the way most Christians live.

For Self.

A more biblical perspective would be that *I belong to Jesus because He paid His life for me*. Therefore, twenty-four hours of every day belong to the Lord, and I have to carve out time to go to work. I actually have to take away time from the Lord's day in order to make a living. And as soon as I come back home, I run back into my secret place to be in His presence once again, because the day is *His*, not mine.

See the difference? One view lives for Self, the other for the Lord.

This change in perspective can alter the way you view *all* of life, and therefore, the way you *live* life.

You'll actually begin to ask the Lord for permission to take away some of *His* time communing with you so that you can cut the grass or go to the grocery store. You will begin living life for Him instead of for yourself.

You adore God because He paid the price for you and you belong to Him.

Everything you have belongs to Him. The One who owns you, calls you to love Him with everything you have within yourself. And as His slave, you are to do the bidding of your Master.

You've seen that an adorer is one who loves God with the deepest and most heartfelt affections while orally acknowledging this great love they have for their God. It is synonymous with loving the Lord your God with all your heart, all your soul, all your strength, and all your mind.

Although obedience is important, you are not to place all of your energy and focus on being obedient to perform the commandments given. Your focus must be to adore God with everything you have within you, and in doing so, obedience to Him will flow naturally *from* you.

We've looked at just a few of the reasons why you should adore God, or why you should become a true, constant, faithful, accurate, and undeviating worshiper.

Adoring God creates intimacy with the God of the universe. He cares for you, loves you, protects you, sustains you at every moment of the day, and this intimate relationship with Him creates a lifestyle where everything that you need is provided for, because He's *with* you.

You have also seen how that kind of close relationship results in you being able to receive revelatory knowledge and instruction on how you should proceed in every area of your life. You will never go wrong by relying on Him. And you are only close enough to hear and receive that instruction by adoring Him with everything you have within you.

We've also delved into the idea that you are not your own, and you were bought with a price. Another reason why you should become a worshiper of God is because He paid the ultimate price to free you from the most cruel master you could ever have and bought you to be a servant to Himself.

Your Master desires, and is seeking after a true, constant, accurate, sincere, and undeviating adorer of God! One who is so overwhelmed with loving Him that he falls down in humble submission while orally acknowledging this great love that he has.

I pray that I have adequately shown you what the heart of a worshiper looks and feels like. It is what touches the heart of God like nothing else.

So, let's put what you've learned back into the context of the verse.

> *John 4:23-24 But the hour cometh, and now is, when the true (the faithful, constant – which is all the time, accurate – according to the standard, and undeviating – never moving from the proper path) worshippers (adorers, those who hold the deepest respect, the highest honor for God, and love Him with all their hearts, and souls, and minds) shall worship the Father in spirit and in truth: for the Father seeketh (is looking for, desiring, bending His efforts towards trying to find) such to worship Him. (vs 24)*

WHAT IS A WORSHIPER?

God is a Spirit; and they that worship Him must (it's mandatory) worship Him in spirit and in truth (the only thing that is always accurate and undeviating wherever you are, and in whatever circumstances you find yourself – the Word of God).

CHAPTER EIGHT

WORSHIP

The next word or concept that I would like you to explore is the topic toward which everything in our verse has been pointing. Worship.

Much can be said concerning this topic. Within the Christian community, there's such varied opinion on what worship means and its scope that hundreds of books have been written to describe its value, which seem to differ slightly with each individual writer.

My intention is to continue as I have started, as directed by 2 Timothy 2:15, rightly dividing, dissecting, and expounding upon individual words within the selected verse.

Quite honestly, if we were attempting to undertake studying a different topic, for example, prophecy or eschatology (end times events), or certain types and shadows and their archetypes throughout Scripture, we would probably need to use a different methodology for gleaning the truth of that topic.

But because we are narrowly focusing on a particular type of worship amidst the many facets that presented themselves in that day, this method of rightly dividing, dissecting, and expounding is the best way to get a true biblical understanding of what this incredible topic means.

There are approximately 12-14 different Greek words, depending upon the translation, that are used in the New Testament for our English word *worship*. And much information can be gleaned when each word is viewed individually and then within their contexts.

The following are the reference numbers in Strong's Exhaustive Concordance for each Greek word translated as 'worship' in the New Testament, for anyone who would like to study them further: 1391, 1479, 2151, 3000, 4352, (4352+1799), 2323, (4573, 4574, 4576, 2318—note that 2318 has a root of Theos—2316, and 4576, so I grouped these all together)—3511, 2356.

My purpose is not to present an overall picture of all the varied forms of worship described throughout Scripture. Our study is solely based upon one Greek word, 'proskuneo' (pronounced praws-koon-eh-oh), in John 4:23-24, for several important reasons.

First of all, *proskuneo* is by far the most used word in the New Testament for the worship due to God. It is used over fifty times, compared to the approximately twenty times that all the other worship words *combined* are used. If for no other reason, the sheer volume of times it is used should make us, as students of God's Word, take special notice of it.

A second reason we are looking into this specific word is that in our Scripture John 4:23 – 24, Jesus said this is the kind of worship the Father is looking for. He could have used any of the other words to describe exactly what the Father desired, but He *chose* to use prokuneo.

We have already seen what the word 'seeks' means and taken note of the fact that it is not a casual seeking or looking for, that is taking place. God is desiring, longing for, bending his efforts toward trying to find, and even craving and demanding this type of worship. Proskuneo.

Therefore, if Jesus chose this specific word—which identifies this particular type of worship—to describe the intense longing of the Father, then we need to give it special attention as well.

Finally, you should think on this: when Jesus was teaching His disciples to pray in Matthew 6:9-13:

> *"He taught them saying,* **9** *In this manner, therefore, pray: Our Father in heaven, Hallowed be Your name.* **10** *Your kingdom come. Your will be done on earth as it is in heaven.* **11** *Give us this day our daily bread.* **12** *And forgive us our debts, as we forgive our debtors.* **13** *And do not lead us into temptation but deliver us from the evil one. For Yours is the kingdom and the power and the glory forever. Amen." (NKJV)*

Most of you will know this prayer and have prayed it many times. But let's look at the first two verses (9-10) again. **9** In this manner, therefore, pray: Our Father in heaven, Hallowed be Your name. **10** Your kingdom come. Your will be done on earth as it is in heaven. Stop.

What are you really saying when you are praying this portion of the prayer? You are saying you want His Will to be done on earth as it already is being done in heaven.

How can you know what's going on in heaven, though—and therefore, what He wants to have accomplished here on earth?

All you have to do is turn to the book of Revelation in the Bible and you can see what's happening in heaven. You can actually get a glimpse of God's Will being done in heaven, and what it looks like.

Check out these few verses. (Revelation 4:6-11, 7:11-12, 11:16, 22:8-9.)

In each instance, they are either worshiping God or being instructed that only God deserves the type of worship being given. This worship activity is happening day and night, twenty-four hours per day, seven days per week.

It never stops!

Actually, it's never really night-time in heaven, and there are no periods of time such as twenty-four hours in a day, or seven days in a week, but you get the idea. It's *constantly* happening!

The *only* kind of worship performed and accepted before God's throne in heaven, is proskuneo.

So, part of His Will that He wants to be done on earth as it is in heaven, is true worship, but not just *any* kind of worship! His Will is for you to prokuneo Him. And that's why He's seeking it.

As I've stated, there are between twelve and fourteen different words used in the New Testament for worship, each one carrying a slightly different meaning or emphasis. For God to consistently use *this* word to describe the activity of heaven is incredibly significant, and then for Jesus to teach His disciples to pray that what we see approved of as God's Will in heaven should also be done on earth, carries powerful significance as well.

Let's look at the verse again.

> *John 4:23-24. "But the hour cometh and now is, when the true worshipers shall worship the Father in spirit and in truth: for the Father seeketh such to*

> *worship Him. God is a Spirit, and they that worship Him must worship Him in spirit and in truth."*

As I mentioned previously, the Greek word used here is listed in the Strong's Concordance (4352) as proskuneo. This word means: to kiss like a dog licking his master's hand; to fawn or crouch, that is, (lit. or fig.) prostrate oneself in homage (do reverence to, adore)—worship.

It should be noted that the previous word for worshiper—'proskunetes'—(praws-koon-net-is; 4353) from the Strong's Concordance, is derived directly from our word here: (4352 prokuneo). Therefore, since the words are directly related etymologically, much of the same directions concerning the condition of the heart and positions of the body are also identical.

The idea of a worshiper, by definition, is focused upon the condition of the heart, one of adoration or great love, the deepest respect, and the highest honor.

The position of the body will always be a secondary concern. But it's a position of humility, submission, and surrender, this condition and position to be displayed publicly, privately, and vocally.

Now let's look at how the Bible describes what the true worshiper (adorer) does.

The worshiper or adorer and lover of God worships Him!

The first definition of proskuneo says, 'To kiss like a dog licking his master's hand.'

I've heard more than a few disgruntled Christians push back at the reference in this definition, asking, "Are we supposed to be the dog in this scenario?" And after I go through the process of calming them down, I answer, "Absolutely!" Then I try to describe what is meant by this word picture.

It's actually a beautiful scene.

Have you ever owned a dog? Have you ever noticed your dog's reaction when you come home? It doesn't matter if you've been gone all day at work, or just left the house for five minutes to go pick up a loaf of bread from the local grocery store; your dog acts like it hasn't seen you in...*forever*, jumping and barking and wagging its tail and licking you! Every part of the dog's body is exuberant with joy because you came into the room.

I had two Airedale Terriers, Bradley and Bailey, that would both go crazy every time I stepped in the door! Now you should understand, most Airedale Terriers only grow to around fifty pounds. But my dogs had been bred differently and so they were taller and heavier than the regular breed, each weighing about ninety to ninety-two pounds!

Jumping was never an issue because they were well-trained. However, whenever I sat on the floor, they somehow thought that either it was time to play, or they magically morphed into twenty-pound lapdogs!

And they could spend hours just licking me and nuzzling up against me as I petted and stroked them and showed them love.

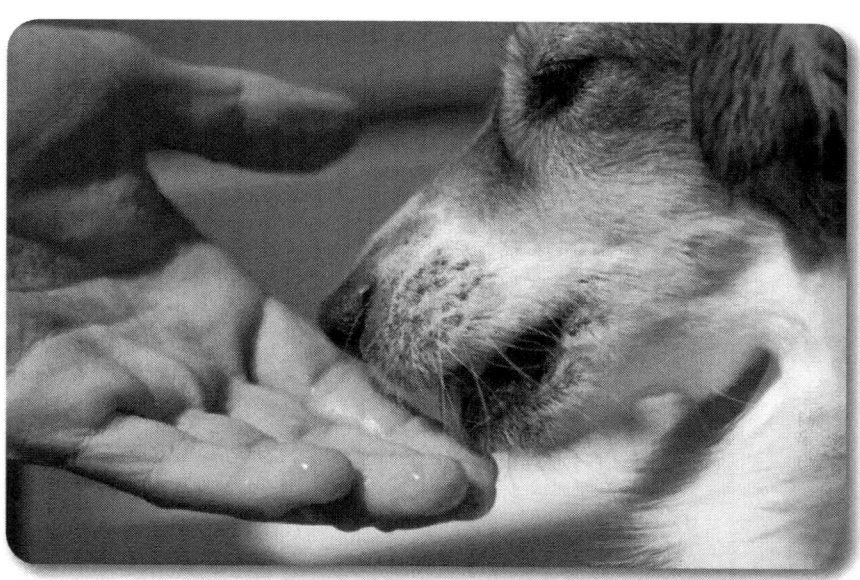

Look at the picture our definition is presenting. "Like a dog licking his master's hand." In reality, a dog doesn't have lips in the way a person does, so licking is in essence *kissing* the master's hand. In most cases, especially with Bradley and Bailey, the dog doesn't stop kissing or licking the master until the master *forces* him to stop. But all the while, that dog is continually showing his affection and his love toward his master with every part of his being. His whole body is moving with excitement, acknowledging that his master is the one who feeds him to keep him alive, who gives the dog fresh water, who provides shelter and warmth, etc.

This is an incredible description of how we are to be toward our Master, who provides all that we need and so much more! This condition of the heart being described contains all the heartfelt genuineness of complete adoration, just as we studied with a worshiper or an adorer, and then adds the element of focused and extreme gratitude. Just like my dogs.

This worship, since it *contains* adoration, has all the inward qualities of such, while also focusing on a physical position as an outward expression of the inward condition of your heart.

That external position is likened to that of a dog. A dog's position is down low, always looking up toward his master for direction. It's a position of humility, submission, and respect for his master. By definition, this is an external downward movement in subjection; fawning, crouching, prostrating oneself in homage.

Therefore, accompanying the heartfelt emotions experienced in worship is always an external or physical expression of that inward feeling. That which was felt internally had an external manifestation mirroring it.

So far, we have the primary condition of unfettered gratitude and heartfelt adoration, like a dog licking his master's hand, and the external positioning of being down low, surrendered and submissive to the Master, crouching, kneeling, fawning, and prostrated in homage.

But there's more!

What does homage mean?

The definition of homage is, 1) a public avowal of allegiance by a vassal to his lord. 2) An act done, or thing given to show the relationship between lord and vassal. Anything given or done to show reverence, honor, or respect.

These concepts are what move proskuneo out from *only* the realm of heartfelt emotion and to include the external aspects of something being done or given while expressing those internal feelings.

Homage is an action performed to show the relationship between a vassal and his lord. A vassal was simply a servant. And many times, the vassals' response when coming into the presence of his lord or master, was a physical sign of submission such as lying prostrate, bowing, or kneeling, crouching, falling upon the knees and then gradually inclining the body until the forehead touched the ground. These are all external expressions of paying obeisance to one of superior station.

As they came before kings, or as a king entered into their presence, the servant would bow down low, get on his knees, or lie prostrate as the king passed by. Their act or position of submission was sufficient to show the king the surrendered attitude, or to expose the heart of his servant.

Now think of your God. He wants the whole of your heart surrendered to Him. This is first and foremost His desire. But if your heart is fully submitted to Him, then the complimentary physical manifestation of that surrendered heart will be an external homage, i.e., a physical expression of that internal condition.

An adorer of God is a worshiper of God, and a worshiper of God worships God in this manner, because only God is worthy of this type of worship.

Let's look at one more portion of our definition for homage. It's a public avowal of allegiance by a vassal to his lord.

What is an avowal? An avowal is an open declaration, frank acknowledgment. And as many of us already know, a declaration is an open expression of facts or opinions; a public annunciation; a proclamation.

Therefore, an avowal is an open declaration or expression of facts and opinions. It is an open proclamation. The definition of avowal says that it is also public.

So, it's a *public* avowal of allegiance. This means that what is given between the vassal toward his lord, has some sort of public expression attached to it to show the relationship between them.

Are you seeing what's taking place?

Let's put some thoughts together before moving on.

To worship God in the manner He prescribes, is to approach Him with the condition of your heart overflowing with gratitude and in the total adoration of your being! This heartfelt state doesn't simply reside *inside* of you. It bubbles up out of your being and contains the external manifestation of physically bowing, kneeling, prostrating yourself in public, while orally acknowledging this great love you have for your King.

The definition says you are to; kiss like a dog licking his master's hand, fawn, or crouch, that is, (lit. or fig.) prostrate oneself in homage (do reverence to, adore)—worship.

To prostrate oneself means; to lie flat or prone, cast oneself down. Lying with the face downward in demonstration of great humility or abject submission, lying completely subjugated; overwhelmed.

To prostrate oneself *in homage* then, means that you are to lie flat or prone, cast oneself down, lying face downward *publicly* as an external expression or demonstration of great humility or abject submission to show the relationship between yourself and your Master.

In each portion of the definition, we see how the heart condition of you pouring out your greatest love, deepest respect, and the highest honor, with extreme gratitude toward the One who provides so much for you, is primary. With your being totally overwhelmed by His greatness and goodness, you fall to your knees, or lie prostrate before Him, orally acknowledging this great love for your God!

Prokuneo envelops all the oral and heartfelt adoration of a true worshiper, along with the surrendered bodily positions which publicly demonstrate your great love and devotion toward your Master.

No other kind of worship known throughout the ancient world compares to the genuineness and subjected display of proskuneo.

Remember, God looks at the heart. The adoration aspect of proskuneo prohibits falsehood. If the heart is not totally and continually engaged, it ceases to be proskuneo, and therefore, ceases being the kind of worship God is desiring.

In other words, you can't fake this.

Many people can't appreciate what's been presented here. They refuse to accept that God would require a *public* demonstration, especially one requiring them to, as some have stated it, 'look stupid'. They wonder what other people who don't practice this, will think. So, they simply say they won't do it, especially if they are in church or another public setting, or if they are dressed in a nice outfit.

To make the point: they are ashamed to do it.

That's a very real obstacle to overcome, and I'm not insensitive in this matter. There were times in the past when I struggled with some of these very same issues. However, here's a thought that I kept close to my heart, that helped me move forward. I pray it helps you as well.

It is this: Jesus was beaten, bruised, and hung *publicly*. He wasn't crucified, as seen in most crucifixion paintings, in a loincloth. He was naked, utterly exposed and vulnerable while the world came by, spit upon Him, and mocked Him.

Take a moment and imagine that!

He wasn't ashamed to die in utter humiliation to show His love for me. Yet I am ashamed to humble myself, and to publicly bow down to show *my* love for Him? Consider this as well; most times we will demonstrate this in church! Will you still be ashamed to love Him and give Him the one thing He is seeking even while among those who claim to love God as we do?

> *Mark 8:38 says, "Whosoever therefore shall be ashamed of me and of my words in this adulterous and sinful generation; of him also shall the son of man be ashamed, when he comes in the glory of His Father with His holy angels".*

This verse of Scripture along with my corresponding actions scared me because it exposed the fact that I was ashamed to publicly worship Him the way He prescribes, for fear of the opinions of others.

However, it also became the sobering thought that brought me out of my selfish carnality and allowed me to put Him, and His desires above my own.

Does this describe you as well? Please think about what He publicly went through *for you*. Then consider that if you are ashamed of Him now, He will be ashamed of you later when He comes in the glory of His Father.

I pray these private thoughts that helped me move past this state of mind are not too harsh for some to receive. My intention is never to be harsh, but to present the truth in love while still containing the fullness and gravity of how I received it.

This is what helped me, and without a doubt, it changed my life and the lives of others who have put it into practice. I sincerely hope it helps you as well.

Let's continue with our study.

> *John 4:23-24 But the hour cometh, and now is, when the true (the faithful, constant – all the time, accurate – correct according to the standard, and undeviating – never moving from the proper path) worshippers (adorers, those who hold the deepest respect, the highest honor for God, and love Him with all their hearts, and souls, and minds) shall worship (Bow themselves down in humble submission, kneel*

> *or prostrate themselves publicly with their body and hearts in subjection to their God, orally declaring the great love they have towards) the Father in spirit and in truth: for the Father seeketh (is looking for, desiring, bending His efforts towards trying to find) such to worship Him. (vs 24) God is a Spirit; and they that worship Him must (it's mandatory) worship Him in spirit and in truth (the only thing that is always accurate and undeviating wherever you are, and in whatever circumstances you find yourself – the Word of God).*

Wow. We've come a long way and gleaned many nuggets of truth from this verse, haven't we?

Can you begin to see how His Word has been "rightly divided", cut apart and dissected, and each word has been expounded upon, and clarified so that you now have more understanding of this topic?

Can you see something revealed that you didn't previously know about true worship?

Think about it. What was it?

Through the rightly divided Word of God, He's showing you *His* way of worship!

And now the only question is, are you willing to give Him worship as *He* designed it to be?

CHAPTER NINE

'IN SPIRIT/SPIRIT'

The last portion of our verse that we want to delve into, is the concept of 'in spirit'.

> *John 4:23 "But the hour cometh, and now is, when the true worshippers shall worship the Father in spirit and in truth: for the Father seeketh such to worship Him. (vs 24) God is a Spirit and they that worship Him must worship Him in spirit and in truth."*

The Strong's Concordance, Spirit, 4151 Pneuma (pnoo-ma); a current of air, i.e. breath (blast) or a breeze; by analogy or figure: a spirit, i.e. (human) the rational soul, (by implication) vital principle, mental disposition. (Superhuman) an angel, demon or (divine) God, Christ's spirit, or the Holy Spirit: ghost, life, spirit,

Thayer's Greek Lexicon adds when speaking of the human spirit; the rational spirit, the power by which a human being feels, thinks, wills, and decides; the soul. When referring to God, it states: a spirit i.e. a simple essence, devoid of all or at least all grosser matter; and possessed of the power of knowing, desiring, deciding, and acting. A life-giving spirit is spoken of Christ as raised from the dead. God is spirit essentially.

We can usually tell from the context, but even if we couldn't, the King James version of the Bible has a neat little way of letting us know whether we are speaking of man's spirit, or God's Spirit. When speaking of God's Spirit, the King James Version uses a capital "S", while when speaking of the spirit of man, it uses a lower-case "s".

That's pretty neat, isn't it? I mean, you could delve deeper into the word 'spirit' to discover the truth for yourself, but it's nice to have little aids to help with understanding.

> *John 4:23-24, "But the hour cometh, and now is, when the true worshippers shall worship the Father in spirit and in truth: for the Father seeketh such to worship Him.(24) God is a Spirit and they that worship Him must worship Him in spirit and in truth."*

Verse 24 starts by saying God is a Spirit. Big 'S'. This is describing God's essence. He is devoid of all or at least all grosser matter and possessed of the power of knowing, desiring, deciding, and acting. He is a life-giving spirit, as is spoken of about Christ when He was raised from the dead.

Another biblical reference I sometimes use is from Barnes New Testament notes. When our definition says God is devoid of all or at least all grosser matter, Barnes notes states that this means that God is spirit essentially and is without a body. He is not material or composed of parts like you and I are, but He is invisible and, in every place, Pure and Holy. He is pure Spirit. This is what is meant by "God is a Spirit".

Barnes notes continues: 'a pure, a holy, a spiritual worship, therefore, is such as he seeks—the offering of the soul rather than the formal offering of the body—the homage of the heart rather than that of the lips.'

This is why God requires a spiritual worship coming from the depths of your heart and encompassing the totality of your being. He wants *all* of you!

This first mention of the word 'spirit'—little 's' in our verse—is referring to the spirit of man, speaking of *our* spirit! That's significant because it means that *we—and by inference, you—have a part to play!* If you just sit back and wait for God to move without taking the initiative and doing something, you'll be waiting a long time!

My spiritual mentor, Pops, used to say, "It's like a standoff. You're waiting for God to move, and God is waiting for *you* to move. The only problem on our side is, God has an eternity to wait!"

There are some occurrences in life when you do need to wait and hear from God to determine the proper direction to go. I understand that. But for the areas such as giving thanks, praise, worship, prayer, reading your Bible, preaching the Gospel, praying for those who are sick and oppressed by the enemy etc., areas the Bible already calls you to move in, there is no need for you to ask for God's direction. These are areas in which you need to move out in faith, knowing that God's Word has already called you to live them.

Worship is one such area.

You are to take the initiative and worship Him with that part of yourself that thinks, and feels, and wills and decides. It's a *purposeful* decision to set your will to say, 'I Will' worship Him! Then you decide or 'will' yourself to attach all your feelings, emotions, and thoughts upon Him. You shut out the world and pour out your heart in submission to Him. And as you begin to initiate those 'spirit' faculties, and you *decide* to place them at the feet of Jesus, something wonderful happens! The Holy Spirit, the Paraclete (pair-a-cleet, or Helper) in Greek, comes alongside to assist you, converting all your best efforts into something acceptable to God.

And God is well pleased.

You should say "*I Will* worship Him" whether you feel like it or not, whether others around think it's crazy, whether the whole world says that it doesn't require all that from you.

They may think it's impractical, and ridiculous, just like the disciples thought about Mary's unrestrained act of worship in Matthew 26. But Jesus said it was an act that was *so* necessary that it had everlasting consequences!

That's why we're all still talking about it today. And as this next biblical story is presented, take some time to consider what Mary had to go through to accomplish worshiping Jesus.

I think you'll find that Mary had the heart of a true worshiper, and that her heart was revealed to all who were there. She worshiped in spirit and truth, no matter what obstacles stood in her way.

> *Matt. 26:6-13: "And when Jesus was in Bethany at the house of Simon the leper, [7] a woman came to Him having an alabaster flask of very costly fragrant oil, and she poured it on His head as He sat at the table. [8] But when His disciples saw it, they were indignant, saying, "Why this waste? [9] For this fragrant oil might have been sold for much and given to the poor."[10] But when Jesus was aware of it, He said to them, "Why do you trouble the woman? For she has done a good work for Me. [11] For you have the poor with you always, but Me you do not have always. [12] For in pouring this fragrant oil on My body, she did it for My burial. [13] Assuredly, I say to you, wherever this gospel is preached in the whole world, what this woman has done will also be told as a memorial to her."*

First of all, this woman was serious about worshiping Jesus. Nothing was going to stand in her way.

'Mary's act of adoration was unreserved in every possible way. She held nothing back!

The financial cost, which was substantial, didn't restrain her. The emotional cost of breaking down in tears before the judgmental eyes of the disciples didn't stop her. Worrying about what those same disciples would say or think about what she was doing didn't hinder her.

Adoring Jesus was her *sole* focus! Nothing was going to keep her from offering Him everything she had, both emotionally and physically; she gave her best! She didn't wait for a better opportunity. She didn't stall or put it off until there may have been a time when she could find Jesus alone. She gave her all, right then and right there. She was totally unreserved! It was desperate. She had to get to Jesus right now! She poured out her all upon Him, not just materially in the ointment, but also in tears. Her heart was completely surrendered!'

Put yourself in Mary's shoes for a moment and ponder these questions.

- How do you express your adoration for Jesus?
- Do you try to show Him anything at all, or do you simply say that "since He knows all things, He already knows how I feel", and leave it at that? Frankly, that's what most of us do.
- Do you show Him in ways that are important to you and that cost you?

It's been stated that the cost of the oil in Mary's jar was the approximate value of one year's wages.

- Would you be so bold as to take something costing a full year's salary and pour it out on Jesus? Or would you consider that wasteful?
- Are you afraid to show your love toward God because of the thoughts or opinions of others around you?

Just putting thought to how you might react under the same conditions, or how you *do* react when faced with similar conditions every Sunday in church, puts Mary's act in a different light, doesn't it?

Now that you know what true worship is and how to give it, falling down on Sunday morning in church and pouring out your heart to God may still seem a bit much to some.

It wasn't for Mary. She gave her all!

'Mary's act wasn't appreciated by everybody in the room. Some saw what she did as completely ridiculous! Matt.26:8 says they "... had indignation..." They got angry about it! They saw it as totally impractical. They felt the practical thing to do would have been to sell the oil and use it to help the poor. But worship (of this type) when we pour ourselves out to Jesus *is* impractical!

It's impractical to spend time going to church when your life is already so busy. It's impractical to spend hours each day in prayer and Bible study when your schedule is completely full!'

What Mary did showed Jesus how much she adored Him no matter how ridiculous or impractical others thought it was. In fact, her pouring out the most expensive item she owned showed Jesus the worth that she placed *on Him* over anything else in life.

That is worship!

'Isn't it about time *you* showed Jesus how much you adore Him, no matter how ridiculous and impractical it may seem to be to others?'

In verses 10-11, Jesus defends what Mary is doing. He says what she did was a good thing. Please understand, 'Jesus wasn't drawing a contrast between helping the poor and worshipping Him - He wasn't saying don't do one in order to do the other. He was saying helping the poor is good in its time and place!' But right now, He's there and the more needful thing in *that* moment of time, was to worship at His feet.

Worshiping Him was a desperate, crucial thing to do because He was right there with them, and she may never get another chance. That was exactly the case. He was about to die and be taken away from them.

The best thing to do is take the time to pour out your everything upon Him right now; sit at His feet and soak in His Words and presence.

You'll have time for good works later. Besides, you need to cultivate intimacy with Him first, because good works like helping the poor mean nothing if you're not doing it out of an overflow of a loving relationship with Jesus Christ.

Remember, if your heart is wrong, your good works are worthless in eternity.

Even atheists run charities.

We stated that Mary's alabaster box and the perfume in it had a certain value. A year's wage!

'Where is that money now? If Mary had kept her box and perfume intact, after all this time it would still be broken and scattered among ruins, buried beneath the sands in the Middle East by now!

'Even if she chose to use it on herself, where would it be? It would be dust!

'Instead, she chose to use it in a way that is eternal. She broke it and poured it out on Jesus, and by doing so, she did something of *eternal* significance.'

In fact, the fragrance of Mary's act of worship and adoration has *never* worn off. That's why we're still talking about it today.

- So, how would you sum up your worship?
- Do those "practical" things take up all your time until you have no time to adore Him? If so, what are you investing your time in? All those "practical" things will eventually turn to dust.
- Are you ready to invest in something eternal?
- Are you ready to unreservedly pour yourself out in worship, and adore Jesus?'

It's time to 'will' yourself to adore Jesus in the most extravagant way you know how. Set your mind, saying, *I 'will' worship Him and nothing, no obstacle, no cost, no impracticality will prevent me from loving Him with all my heart, all my soul, all my mind and all my strength.*

This type of adoring worship is eternal.

As you can see, Mary *willed* herself to worship Christ. She must have said to herself, 'It doesn't matter what it cost. It doesn't matter what it looks like. It doesn't matter if others think I'm foolish, or that the things that I'm doing seem unnecessary or ridiculous. I *will* find a way to worship Him.'

She took that part of herself that thinks, and feels, and wills, and decided that nothing would stop her from getting to Jesus' feet. *This* is the vital importance of understanding this portion of 'in spirit'.

Your spirit, that part of you that decides, and 'wills', must now make a choice to put the desires of your selfish nature down! Make that carnal nature bend to your will. Kill it! It doesn't matter if you're tired, when you don't feel like it, when the flesh just says 'no'. You *must* make the decision to get rid of everything that's hindering you, because you've got to worship and get into the presence of God. Pour out your heart in desperation and let *nothing* stand in the way of getting to God!

This is what God desires.

And that is how you employ your whole heart. That is what 'in spirit' entails.

> *John 4:23-24: But the hour cometh, and now is, when the true (the faithful, constant – all the time, accurate – correct, and undeviating – never moving from the proper path) worshipers (adorers, those who hold the deepest respect, the highest honor for God, and love Him with all their hearts, and souls, and minds) shall worship (bow themselves down in humble submission, kneel or prostrate themselves publicly*

with their body and hearts in subjection to their God, orally declaring the great love they have toward) the Father in spirit (that part of them that thinks, feels, wills, and desires) and in truth: for the Father seeketh (is looking for, desiring, bending His efforts towards trying to find) such to worship Him. (vs 24) God is a Spirit (He's pure essence, not composed of material parts, but a pure and Holy Spirit essentially); and they that worship Him must (it's mandatory. If you're going to worship Him, it's mandatory that you do it in this way) worship Him in spirit and in truth (the always accurate and undeviating wherever you are and in whatever circumstances you find yourself – the Word of God).

CHAPTER TEN

THE TABERNACLE OF MOSES

(The Difference Between Thanksgiving, Praise, and Worship)

"Enter into His gates with thanksgiving, into His courts with praise, be thankful unto Him and bless His name." Psalms 100:4

Sticking to our format from 2 Timothy 2:15, you've seen how knowing the meaning of keywords in a verse can greatly amplify your understanding. Let's look at Psalms 100:4, with some keywords in Hebrew brought out. "Enter into His gates with thanksgiving (towdah), into His courts with praise (tehillah), be thankful (yada) unto Him and bless (barak) His name."

This verse beautifully depicts the Tabernacle of Moses from the book of Exodus, and how you are to come into God's presence. Therefore, it also describes how you are to come into His presence while approaching church on a Sunday morning, or prayer time in your secret closet at home, or *wherever* you seek to enter God's presence.

TRUE WORSHIP: THE GATEWAY TO INTIMACY WITH GOD

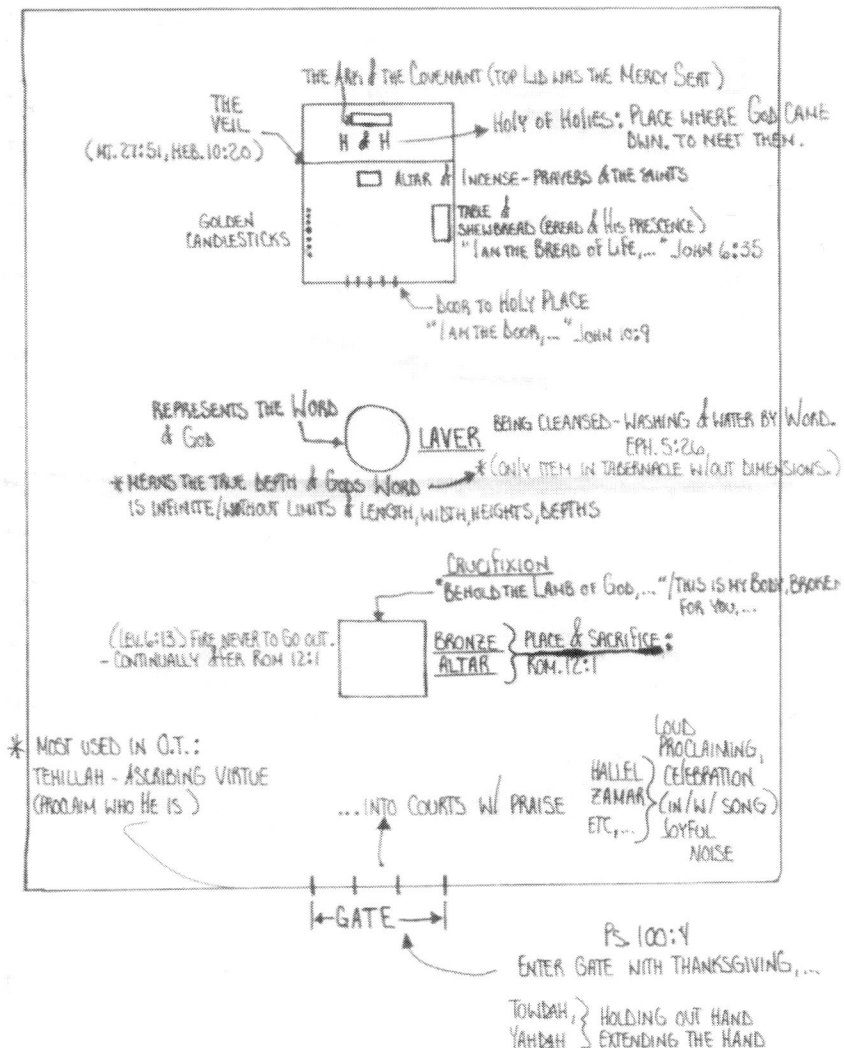

You enter His gates with thanksgiving. The Hebrew word used for thanksgiving used here is towdah (pronounced toe-duh), which is related to the second Hebrew word used for thanks: yada (pronounced yah-dah).

Towdah and Yada, (thanks/thanksgiving) have as their root meaning: to extend the hands.

Combining the translation and meaning of both words, you can see that the heart you should have is an attitude of gratitude and thankfulness, while you are extending or raising hands to the Lord.

Again, we're confronted with the truth that what you are to give God contains both a condition of the heart, and a position of the body.

As it is in worship, it is also essential here to recognize the importance of the internal condition, and physical positioning in thanksgiving. The condition of the heart must always have the primary focus of your attention. But the position of your body, although always secondary, cannot be ignored.

You need to understand that you are not simply a physical being, nor are you solely comprised of pure spiritual essence like God. You are a tri-part being consisting of body, soul, and spirit. And God has made you in such a way that you cannot easily separate the parts of one without affecting the others.

What you've learned about being a true worshiper, and worship itself, proves that the inward condition of your heart bubbles up and flows outward in external physical manifestations. Who you are on the inside moves you to act on the outside.

Some espouse the idea that the opposite has merit as well, that what you do *externally* can also affect you *internally*. They say you can see this influence through the Hebrew words used for thanksgiving, towdah and yada.

Jerry Wyrick, President of Worship Arts Conservatory, says this concerning the many psychological studies about the things people do and how they affect our feelings, emotions, and states of mind.

"It is difficult to be happy while wearing a frown or sad while smiling. There are certain postures that open us up emotionally and others that close us down.

"Our emotions are tied to our muscles.

"When we take an open posture, our emotions also open up. Our physical and spiritual parts are connected in such a way that our actions can change our hearts and our emotions can affect our actions.

"Some of you are afraid of what others might think, so first give it a try in private. Try praising God with hands crossed in front of you and head down. Then try it with arms wide open and head raised to God. You will *feel* different."

I believe this is true, and it's a great exercise for Christians who are somewhat reserved in their expressions of praise toward God. Try it from time to time and take note of any differences. It may help you open up emotionally in giving thanks to God.

Please understand, the Bible doesn't say that what is on the outside will *definitely* change you on the inside. But vice-versa *does* apply. What's inside *will* come out!

"From the abundance of the heart, the mouth speaks."

Remember, Jesus said,

"With their lips they worship me, but their hearts are far from me."

They were doing and saying things that would seem to express their devotion externally, while their internal faith was misplaced somewhere else.

However, if your heart is agreeing with the truth concerning thanksgiving and praise, and you realize your need and desire to change, then practice extending your hands deliberately and with intention, and purposely vocalize thanks to God. You *can* allow the external to affect you internally.

But notice, this is something that happens when you already have the proper heart attitude, that inward condition of gratitude toward God and all He has done for you. Then you desire to perform the external.

The internal still comes first.

When you are already a believer and desire a closer relationship in your daily walk with God, but you're hesitant to publicly extend your arms in an open posture to heaven in thankfulness to God, *that* is when this can help. That is why all Christians, especially those very reserved in their times of thanksgiving, praise, and worship, should set their minds upon all that God has done for them, and in their private times, practice the open postures of thanksgiving. You *will* feel different!

Such is the power of the connection between your spirit, soul, and body.

Let's now look a little closer at thanksgiving.

Most of you will understand the idea of a blood sacrifice or blood offering because this is what Jesus paid for our—and your—sins! But few of you, comparatively, may be familiar with the idea of a sacrifice or an offering of *thanksgiving*. In the Old Testament, a thank-offering was not given because of sin, but as an overflow of gratitude for all God had done in their lives. And if you're not already accustomed to consistently thanking God, you will quickly understand that thankfulness *is* actually a sacrifice! In the beginning, it will feel like a sacrifice to speak things that you are not accustomed to speaking to God. In the beginning of your journey toward a thankful heart, it may be a struggle to recall the things that God has done in your life for which you are thankful.

But take heart! The more you thank Him, the more sensitive you will be in acknowledging the little things in life that He has given to you, things that perhaps you have taken for granted.

And your thankful heart will naturally grow within you.

The importance of thanksgiving cannot be overstated if you're seeking to enter God's presence. You have to learn to continually offer the thanks and appreciation exemplified in these two Hebrew words, towdah, and yada.

Here is why it's so necessary.

Thanksgiving directs your mind to focus on God's provision in your life. So many times, we go through the day living our lives without ever acknowledging the many gifts and benefits that God has provided. Many times, the issues or problems in life take center stage, and we place such emphasis *on them* that all the wonderful things God has done and continues to do—and has promised to continue doing—go unrecognized.

A heart of Thanksgiving fixes that. As you become more thankful for God's goodness, the heart condition of gratitude will bubble up within you. Your focus then switches from the problems of life, to God's wonderful provision for your life, and you become more peaceful, joyful, and receptive to His Spirit's leadings.

It will really do most of us a lot of good to sit down, calm ourselves, and take inventory of all the good things in our lives. We need to recognize that it is God who provides. Without Him, none of it would be possible. Scripture tells us in James 1:17 that:

"Every good and perfect gift is from above, and comes down from the Father of lights, with Whom is no variableness, neither shadow of turning"

This means every good thing in your life has come from God. Everything. That's why He alone is worthy of your thankfulness. Think about what you've learned so far. This is how you're to approach

His presence. Not haughtily or thinking you're due some honor, but humbly.

You enter into His gates with your heart brimming with gratitude and thankfulness, while your arms are raised toward heaven in recognition of God as your provider and sustainer.

This is how you *should* come to church! Not griping about the traffic, but with thanksgiving. Thanking Him for waking you up another day. For food in your stomach, clothes on your back, and a roof over your head. Thanks should permeate your heart and focus your mind upon God as you enter into the court with His congregation.

Giving Praise

The next part of our verse says, "...into His courts with praise (tehillah, pronounced teh-hee-lah)..."

The place you come to after entering the gate of the Tabernacle is the Outer Court. You should now begin to have praise on your lips, not out of obligation or some robotic sense that this is the next necessary step to get to where you are going, but instead because thankfulness and the goodness of God have *so* filled your heart and mind, that praise simply flows from you naturally.

Many of the words used in the Old Testament for praise are celebratory ones that ascribe His virtues and state how glorious He is!

It should be noted that with both thanksgiving and praise, there *can* be aspects that include singing. You are to use *all* of your faculties to give God thanks and praise, and sometimes, this includes singing!

It is not the methods employed to fulfill each type of offering that I am focusing on at this time, but the inner workings of each will be examined.

Some of the main words used in the Hebrew Bible for praise are tehillah, shabach, zamar, and hallel.

'Tehillah', (tih-he-lah), laudation which is the giving of praise, bestowing, or expressing devotion. Its secondary meaning includes singing songs or hymns.

'Zamar', pronounced zah-mar, is a word containing singing as well as playing instruments for the purpose of praising or boasting in God. 'Tehillah' and 'zamar' and our understanding of them are the primary reasons we sing songs or hymns and play instruments in most modern churches today.

'Shabach', pronounced sha-bah-k, is a loud boisterous praise. This is where you are loudly and unashamedly boasting the greatness of your God!

'Halal', pronounced hal-al, means: to make a show, boast, and thus to be clamorously foolish: to celebrate; to praise, to rave, etc.," and it is actually the root word for our first word for praise, 'tehillah'.

So, when giving praise (tehillah, or halal), you are to boast, make a show, and express your devotion to the Lord loudly or in a celebratory manner. Halal is part of a larger word used almost all the time in Christian churches: Hallelujah! Halal (praise) and Yah (short for Yahweh, an Old Testament name for the Most High God*)*. Together, they mean praise Yahweh, praise God, or praise the Lord!

Hallelujah, then, means to boast, shine brightly and act like a fool in praising God! And it's always done in a loud, boasting, celebratory manner. The Bible says that when Israel praised God, the nations heard it! That gives you an idea of the decibel levels!

There's actually a descriptive part of the definition of halal that says, to shine forth, to brightly flash. And since halal is the root word of tehillah, this shining forth and bright flashing applies to it as well. Words that bring images to the mind like these, make me wonder if this is describing what is seen in the spiritual realm when you give God these kinds of praise.

Scriptures talk about putting on the garment of praise (tehillah) for the spirit of heaviness (Isaiah 61:3). If you've ever experienced a heaviness or sadness, and began to praise God in the midst of it, you know that the heaviness lifts and soon afterwards, your entire perspective shifts away from the issue, and toward reliance upon God. I wonder if when you praise in this manner, proudly and unashamedly boasting in your Lord, if God, who inhabits, or is actually enthroned upon the praises (tehillah) of His people (Psalms 22:3), comes to your rescue, and the demonic forces wishing to oppress you cannot stand within the bright, shining light of God which blazes forth from you, and they have to flee! This would be why the sadness or depression you previously had dissolves away. Although I have never fully studied the spiritual portion of this concept in depth, it perfectly fits what you experience, and what happens when you praise God.

Thanksgiving, Praise, and the Flesh

Both thanksgiving and praise are incredible spiritual weapons you can use to combat what the enemy is throwing at you. However, you should be advised that as good and powerful as they are, both can contain a very deceitfully negative aspect of the fleshly or carnal nature. I say it's negative because God hates anything of the flesh.

It's deceitful because unless your mind has been renewed to the Word of God, your heart can still be in the condition of being deceitfully wicked, and the Bible says if that's the case, you can't fully know the depths of the wickedness in your own heart. You need a renewal to take place, or you require that God break that out of your life. Therefore, the unrenewed and unbroken heart, even while fixed upon the thanksgiving and praises of God, can still have deeply carnal motivations which then spoil what could have been a truly spiritual endeavor.

"A little leaven, leavens the whole lump."

All it takes is a little bit of yeast, and it will grow and move throughout the entire loaf. The same can be said of your sinful, fleshly nature which can permeate even the most Godly, spiritual practices, causing them to be done for naught. Because we've never been trained to identify our carnal natures, we are not aware of the power the flesh can exert over us. Therefore, we remain unaware when carnality creeps into our church services, and when the presence of God, who despises anything of the flesh, departs.

This spoiling of Godly endeavors can take place because both thanksgiving and praise are *living* celebrations.

What I mean by 'living celebrations' is that they can be attached to and even controlled by your carnal or fleshly nature. It's alive and well in all of us, and until it's put down, broken, or destroyed, it can control us! It's that part of us that is in opposition to God, that even while performing biblical practices, can materialize so Self can be uplifted. You might not want to hear this, but as you are extending your hands and thanking Him for what He's done, and then loudly celebrating, singing, dancing, or vocalizing your praises for Him, all of which are biblical, an element of flesh that stinks in the nostrils of a Holy God can sneak in and destroy your service to Him. For example, how difficult would it be to dance before the Lord, while people are watching?

For most people, it's exceedingly difficult. The act of performing for God may not be such a dire undertaking, but the fact that you are being seen by others *may* influence you to become people-conscious instead of God-conscious. And you start wondering, "How did I look? Was I on beat?" Or if singing, "How did I sound?"

The deceitfulness of our natural man says, "I just want to give God my best. Therefore, the only responsible thing to do is to concern myself with ancillary characteristics such as practicing endlessly until my voice sounds perfect, or go over the message I'm to deliver until it has just the right tone and/or emotional impact."

So, the song becomes more important than God. The dance becomes more important than God. The message you deliver and how you are perceived in their eyes of other people becomes more important than God.

If you're not careful, the carnality of the flesh will soon have deceived you into placing more worth upon the performance and your perception, than on your outpouring in ministry to God!

Here's something that may shock you; God is not interested in your song, your dance, your message that you worked on for forty hours all week to prepare, unless it is wholly and unreservedly *for Him and Him alone*, not some mixture of Him sharing a portion of His Glory with you.

Every time you adjust the amplifiers to emit a more 'soulful' sound, give your voice a certain vibrato or momentum to signal that you are moving in the anointing of the Holy Ghost, preaching and framing a message to impress the audience, or *anything* that is done to play upon the emotional responses of those around you, constitutes the flesh. That which is done to subtly persuade others that there is something special about you or what you're doing, is the glorification of Self!

Here's a litmus test. What is your first thought after 'performing' for the Lord? For many, their first thought is, "I wonder how that sounded. I wonder what people thought of my song or my dance?"

The desire to be the center of attention, or to be seen, or to be regarded as more spiritual in some way, are all facets of the fleshly nature which long to be praised and admired instead of, or alongside God.

Is this you?

If it is, I don't want this to be as if I'm coming down hard on anyone, but you may want to check your motives.

Are you doing it solely for God and His Glory, or is it ok to get a little glory and acclamation for yourself along the way? This is a way-marker for the flesh, a red flag that something inside may be desiring to steal a little of what was only meant for God.

Is your first thought after your 'performance', "What did God think? Was he pleased with what I presented to Him?" Then perhaps you're on the right track.

You simply need to know that the flesh has a character that is opposed to God and longs to be given glory *alongside* God. Therefore, anything inside you that starts getting 'puffed up' because of the accolades coming from those who enjoy your endeavors for God, must be displaced from your life immediately.

These false anointings, psychological methods, and all human wisdom *must* be put down, not only in your thanksgiving and praise, but in every part of your life.

Scripture says in 1 Corinthians 1:29:

> *"No flesh shall glory in His sight".*

God put provisions in place that would prevent *anything* insinuating of fleshly effort.

> *Ezekiel 44:17-18: "When they enter the gates of the inner court, they are to wear linen garments; they must not wear anything made of wool when they minister at the gates of the inner court or inside*

> *the temple. 18 They are to wear linen turbans on their heads and linen undergarments around their waists. They must not wear anything that makes them perspire."*

The priests ministering in the Tabernacle had to wear linen garments. Anything other than linen, and the priests would sweat. And sweating signaled human effort. God wanted *nothing* of human effort contaminating His sacrifices.

> *Exodus 20:26 "Nor shall you go up by steps to My altar, that your nakedness may not be exposed on it."*

The priests had to go up the altar to offer sacrifices on a ramp, not on steps. On steps, each leg had to be lifted higher, and a portion of the flesh, although it may only be a toe or portion of the foot, may be seen. Going up the altar on a ramp, with their garments dragging on the ground, prohibited the opportunity for any flesh to be seen!

God hates the flesh. He made sure this hatred was well-known and placed within the Laws specific commands that governed how they approached Him. They practiced modesty in every area of life to, at least outwardly, show God they complied with His wishes. Does that sound like how we live as modern-day Christians?

Or do we purposefully practice exactly the opposite of modesty and endeavor to show as much flesh as possible, just like the rest of the ungodly world?

Knowing God's hatred for all things of the flesh, how do you think He feels about the Church in America?

I was horrified to see older teenage girls in church dressed in those super-short shorts called "Daisy Dukes", and others in yoga pants so tight that they literally left nothing to the imagination. A friend of mine noticed it as well and mentioned it to me, saying the parents were simply happy to have their kids in church.

I could understand that but where was the reverence for the House of God?

There was a time when even if you were living in a way that was opposed to God, if you ever walked into the church for service, you knew enough or had enough respect to dress as modestly as possible. There was a standard called the Word of God that the Church used to live by, so that those entering respected those values, even if that respect was only external and temporary while they attended service.

Not so much anymore. It seems in every part of our Christian lives today, that we're happy with simply living the bare minimum required to make it to heaven.

But is living this way and going through the motions enough?

Please understand, I'm not putting these church girls or their parents on trial.

I don't have a heaven or hell to put anyone into. But this occurrence, along with many others I could mention where our flesh runs rampant, exemplifies the slippery slope the Church has been on and shows how far removed from the heart of God many have become.

Think about all you've learned thus far concerning the condition of your heart manifesting externally into your actions.

Don't judge people, just think about it.

If what is on the outside—the way you dress, speak, interact, etc.—is only manifested from that which is bubbling up and overflowing from within the heart, what does that say about your heart? If you dress immodestly in church without even the *thought* that anything is improper or disrespectful, what do you think your internal state looks like to God?

Many Christians say that they have God shining on the inside of them, but what keeps coming out in their actions is irreverence. With what we've studied in the Scriptures concerning what's inside of us coming out in our actions, can that statement possibly be true? Of course not!

Matthew 6:23 says, "...If therefore the light that is in thee be darkness, how great is that darkness!"

How do you say that you love God, and yet do the things that He hates?

Jesus said,

"With their lips do they worship me, but their hearts are far from me."

We need reverence to return to the House of God.

But let's go back and look where thanksgiving and praise have brought us. This is where we are in our outline of the Tabernacle. We're through the door and the outer court. We now stand before the place where flesh has to die.

Reverence returns at the Brazen Altar.

"Bless"

TRUE WORSHIP: THE GATEWAY TO INTIMACY WITH GOD

The final word in our verse that we're going to look at is the Hebrew word for 'bless', which is barak (pronounced baw-rawk). Barak is a root word that has as its primary meaning, to kneel; by implication, it means to bless God (as an act of adoration) or man (as a benefit). When referencing a person, it means "to bless" or benefit someone. Many times, in Scripture, God is spoken of as blessing His people.

But in our verse Psalms 100:4, barak is used in its most common form as something you are doing for God. This means you're kneeling down as an act of adoration, and here again, you see the condition of the heart (adoration), and position of the body (kneeling).

Barak is similar to the primary Hebrew word in the Old Testament used for worship, Shachah, (pronounced sha-kaw). And shachah is the Old Testament equivalent of our New Testament word that you've already studied, proskuneo. Therefore barak, shachah, and proskuneo are nearly synonymous in many of their meanings.

When the Psalmist says in Psalms 103:1:

> *"Bless the Lord, oh my soul, and all that is within me, bless His holy name,"*

he's saying, 'I will kneel down in adoration, pouring out my heart unto the Lord, and everything else within me (my mind, my will, my strength, my everything!) will kneel down in humble submission and adoration as well, in recognition of His holy name!'

> *Ps 34:18 says, "I will bless the Lord at all times, His praise shall continually be on my lips."*

Many churches use this popular verse for teachings concerning the praising of God for all His wonderful works. That's great! You need to praise Him continually. But the first part of the verse says to 'bless the Lord at all times', so that's barak as well. David is saying that he will kneel down before the Lord in adoration at all times.

It's literally *everywhere* in Scripture.

Keep these definitions in mind when you're reading through the Old Testament and come across the word 'bless', because more often than not, especially if you're reading through the Psalms, 'bless' will be the word barak. And if the object of this adoration is God, then what is required from the giver is both a condition of the heart, and a position of the body. Just as in our New Testament true worship.

Let's put our new understanding of the word 'bless' back into the context of Psalms 100:4.

"Enter into His gates with thanksgiving (towdah – the condition of the heart being an attitude of gratitude while bodily extending or raising the hands), into His courts with praise (tehillah – laudation, bestowing or expressing devotion. Includes singing songs or hymns; and it *can* be loud, boisterous and celebratory), be thankful (yada – set your heart upon thankfulness) unto Him and bless (barak – physically kneel down as an act of (adoration) great love and deepest devotion to) His name." Ps 100:4

This is why I love Word studies. They bring out so much more depth from the pages of Scripture.

After entering His gates with thanksgiving and into His courts with praise, you have fixed your mind upon your God and filled your heart with the wonder of who He is. But now you arrive at the Brazen Altar, and as you all know, the Altar was the place of death. Look at where you are in the Tabernacle! The presence of God dwells in the Most Holy Place, beyond the Veil. You have to move back beyond the Laver, and into the Holy Place to get to Him. God's presence is where you desire to be. But something has to die before you can move any farther.

You've seen that thanksgiving and praise, as powerful as they can be, are what led you into the gates of the Tabernacle, and into the court to place you on the Altar to die.

As thanksgiving and praise are living celebrations, worship is a death process.

Here is where you have to die to self to move any closer to God.

This is where true worship connects and intertwines with the sacrifice on the altar. You've got to die. Selfish ambitions, selfish desires, selfish pride, *me, me, poor, poor me,* has to die!

All your dreams and goals in life have to be surrendered. *Your* way of doing things has to be submitted to God and to *His* way. All that you are has to die on the altar. Then you can come alive in Him.

This is one of the main reasons the Church has moved away from true worship in favor of thanksgiving, praise, or simply singing songs. No one wants to die.

I don't really blame them. Dying hurts.

It hurts to give up those closely held hopes and dreams you had for your life. As you can see, dying as a sacrifice on the altar requires the utmost faith and utter submission to God. Faith is required in that it is virtually unknown what God will do with your life; you have to trust Him and His Plan *more than* trusting yourself and your own plans, and I'd be lying if I told you it was easy.

At least, not at first.

But once you see the goodness of God and are convinced that His way is the best way for your life, surrender becomes easier. But in God's economy, dying is the only way for you—for any of us—to truly live!

The Brazen Altar speaks of sacrifice. It speaks of death. Therefore, it speaks of worship. And worship is how reverence can return to the House of God. This Brazen Altar worship is about willingly surrendering your *all* as a sacrifice to God. I used to think giving God your all and your best meant wearing your fanciest clothes or becoming more active in church by joining the choir, teaching Bible class, etc. But now I realize it's about surrendering all your heart, and all your soul, and all your mind, and all your strength, all your hopes, and all your dreams to Him. It's dying to all you are and placing yourself as a sacrifice at His feet. That is what He desires and is actively looking for.

Through our Bible verse (Psalms 100:4) and Tabernacle depiction, you can see that the purpose of thanksgiving and praise is to focus your heart upon Him, and bring you to the place of death where you can die to self. And in dying to yourself and leaving all your burnt flesh on the Brazen Altar of sacrifice, you are spiritually ushered back past the Laver, through the Holy Place, and into God's presence before the throne.

This is the ultimate goal of true spiritual worship.

So, you see that you have a blueprint of sorts that if followed, can help in your approach to enter into His presence. Thanksgiving leads to praise, which culminates in worship!

You thank Him for all that He's done in your life. "Thank you, Lord, for waking me up this morning, for food on the table and clothes on my back, for the life pulsing through my body, etc." Then you begin praising or proclaiming His virtues. "You're so awesome, God, you're my strength and the One I run to when I'm afraid or in trouble. You never let me down, You've been so good to me..." And when your heart is brimming with gratitude for all He's done, you fall down in acknowledgment of all His greatness and pour out your heart in surrender to Him in worship.

This is the difference between thanksgiving, praise, and worship. And He's created you perfectly fitted to give each of them to Him! You can '*will*' yourself to give each to God in the way He specifies.

The Tabernacle, and Psalms 100:4 describes the journey you take, and what is required to move into His presence.

Will you give Him all He requires for you to come into intimate communion with Him?

David cried out, "What can I render for all Your benefits?" What can I do to give back for all that You've done for me in my life?"

My answer is, you can give everything you are and everything you have. The most comprehensive expression of this is found when you worship Him in spirit and in truth.

We enter into His gates with thanksgiving, and into His courts with praise. We stay thankful having our hearts brimming with gratitude and then humbly bow down in surrendered adoration.

The Tabernacle of Moses gives us His blueprint.

CHAPTER ELEVEN

WORSHIP AND HIS PRESENCE

You began a new relationship with Christ when you got saved, right?

"Well, now I'm a son or daughter, I experience His presence every day."

TRUE WORSHIP: THE GATEWAY TO INTIMACY WITH GOD

I hear this type of comment often when speaking about entering into the presence of God. And they are true statements. Because of your new status as sons and daughters of God, you *can* experience Him every day. You *can*, but unfortunately, I'm not sure many of us do. Especially not in the way we're going to talk about now.

His *intimate* presence.

You *do* have a new relationship as a son or daughter when you become a Christian. But most Christians never learn that there are more incredible experiences in God waiting for them, so they never feel the need to press in and seek Him for more.

Salvation is just the beginning.

Here's an example. Many of you feel as if you've been running this race called life, and then God gets a hold of you, you accept Christ, and *boom*, you cross the finish line called Salvation and can celebrate as Christians.

You're elated, and with good cause! This is an awesome day in your life!

You begin to say like Paul, *I've run the race, I've finished the course, I put up a good fight, and I'm going to get my eternal reward.*

Unfortunately, God is saying "Hey guys, that's not the race."

In reality, what just happened was that you've just walked up to the starting line, and you hear God saying, "*This* is the race! Get ready. Get set. Go!"

You have the rest of your life to run this race; Salvation is just the beginning. It's the starting line. There's a whole new world of sanctification yet to be experienced.

Just as with everything else in Christ, there are service-level aspects to your Christian life, as well as deeper waters in which you can swim. It depends on exactly how deep you want to go to experience God's Presence.

Salvation then, is just touching that outermost layer of experiencing God. As you run this race, you find that you can have a much deeper, more intimate relationship with Him.

Most Christians go through life never hearing that *after* salvation, God still longs for yet more intimacy. Or that He actually desires to enter into your physical space and allow you to commune with Him while He overwhelmingly loves on you! Therefore, we don't understand that there's more to be experienced, so we never feel the need to press in and seek God for more.

Many Christians are being taught that anything more than what the 'experts' deem the 'normative Christian experience' is hyper-emotional, hyper-Pentecostalism, and is to be avoided at all costs. There's a whole generation of new young pastors coming out of seminary who were also taught that these experiences, *because* they are so emotional, should be avoided! It is this fear of becoming too emotionally involved in your worship experience that has robbed us of the deeper and more rewarding life we could be living in Christ.

Unfortunately, these same new pastors, seminarians, and theologians touting these falsehoods have gained a great deal of intellectual knowledge concerning Scripture, without ever having actually experienced spending time in God's Presence.

What a shame!

And since the Church has followed along with how the world operates, giving titles, positions, and prestige to those with the longest string of letters behind their names rather than those who have actually spent time with God, we end up with a *blind leading the blind* situation.

And the Church has fallen into a ditch.

I believe this is one of the reasons why the Church in America has no power.

Why don't we see miracles, and *more* healings, and have supernatural experiences with the Lord to bring to the Church each week to edify the Body?

The answer is, you haven't spent time abiding in His presence. When you do, you'll find that all that He is will permeate your being until you have become more like Him, and the supernatural experiences will naturally begin to flow from those intimate encounters.

You should understand that you've never been taught or shown that there's a life far more powerful, far more glorious, far more triumphant in Christ that you should be living! And since far too few of those who teach you have entered into that Most Holy Place and experienced His life-altering presence for themselves, you have very few spiritual leaders to look to, or to show you that a deeper walk with God even exists.

Remember our Tabernacle depiction?

Admittedly, we all like to hang out in the courts where thanksgiving and praise reign. Seems more fun out there; it's a party! There is singing, and dancing, and loud and boisterous celebrations that don't necessarily force any changes upon you. *That's* why you're more comfortable there.

And this is where most of the saints of God remain.

Remember, your place in the Tabernacle is now directly before the Brazen Altar. The place of sacrifice and death. The place of worship.

There's no way to advance any further without the death of Self, and the total surrender of the heart of the worshiper. You've got to realize that God's Presence is beyond the court, beyond the altar, beyond the laver, even beyond the Holy Place, and into the place called the Holy of Holies.

Your heart should be longing to enter that Most Holy Place! That's where God is. That's what the one Christian desire should be; to minister to God there, to live there, to abide continually in His presence.

Worship, the sacrifice of Self and utter surrender of all that you are, ushers you into the very Presence of God!

The Presence of God

Many have said that since God is Omnipresent, you are in His presence at all times. Technically speaking, that's absolutely correct. He *is* everywhere at the same time.

But part of the issue lies in how you define God's presence.

Most of us believe that since we're already in God's omnipresence, there is nothing more to seek after. Why seek after what you already have?

What most have never considered is that there are many different *types* of God's presence.

The Church's lack of understanding that there are separate types of God's Presence, has kept them blindly thinking that they don't need to seek after all that God offers. And therefore, they've remained ignorant of the many benefits of true worship and the intimacy that ensues with further seeking Him.

Let's look at a Scripture and ponder the implications concerning God's omnipresence.

> *Colossians 1:16-17," For by Him all things were created that are in heaven and that are on earth, visible and invisible, whether thrones or dominions or principalities or powers. All things were created through Him and for Him.* [17] *And He is before all things, and in Him all things consist."*
>
> *"...in Him all things consist."*

The word 'consist' means in the Greek to cohere or hold together. What this means is that not only is God the creator of the universe, and that He existed before anything else came into being, but also that at the most foundational level in this natural world, even on the subatomic level, He is there holding all things together!

This is omnipresence.

This type of His presence is experienced by every person living in the world today. It's Him sustaining every molecule in existence that allows you to live, and move, and breathe. In fact, He's holding together every atom, at every moment, that coheres the makeup of every portion of our entire universe.

Wow. That's incredible!

But His omnipresence isn't the type of presence we're talking about when we refer to entering into the presence of God.

Many stumble in their thinking because they want to think of Him with human characteristics, but He's not totally like us. We're required to be either present in one particular geographical location, or another.

He's not limited in that same way. He can reveal Himself to different persons on opposite sides of the world at the same time, not just because of His omnipresence, but in much more powerful ways.

And each time He appears, He can reveal Himself in singular or multiple forms, and with an infinite number of varying intensities. Just writing about it now, the realization is dawning of the impossibility of adequately describing an encounter with the Most High God of the universe. I just don't have the vocabulary!

Suffice it to say that there are multiple ways God can reveal Himself to you, each unique revelation showing a peculiar *type* or characteristic of who He is.

Here's one type of His presence:

> *Psalm 97:3-5*: "A fire goes before Him and burns up His enemies round about. 4 His lightnings enlightened the world: the earth saw, and trembled. 5 The hills melted like wax at the presence of the Lord, at the presence of the Lord of the whole earth."

Look at what this is saying. A fire issues forth and before He even gets to where He's going, His enemies are destroyed! He steps onto a hillside, and the ground He walks upon melts like wax! That's intense!

Have you ever experienced Him this way? I haven't.

But that is *one type* of His presence.

> <u>Isaiah 64:1</u> *"... that the mountains might quake at your presence."*

Can you imagine this? As the Almighty God approaches, the mountains begin to shake! Those are very drastic, very intense, and powerful manifestations of God's Presence. He can, but He doesn't always appear that way. He can come in exceptionally soft and subtle ways as well.

> <u>Matthew 18:20</u>: *"For where two or three are gathered in My name, there am I in the midst of them."*

What is He doing in this type of His presence? Many times when two or three Christians gather, He's simply drawing them together, and you experience a familial type of love and fellowship that says, "That person is my brother, or my sister" and you're spiritually drawn together as God's family.

Most of us have felt this before. It's incredibly soft, quiet, and unassuming. That's God's presence softly bringing together members of His family!

Let's pause here for a moment. You've seen examples of two different types of His presence. One very comforting, drawing people together as a family, while the other has the ground that He stands on quaking or melting like wax. *Both* are God's Presence being revealed to man.

Here's another example:

> *"And he was transfigured before them, and his face shone like the sun, and his clothes became white as light." Matthew 17:2*

This is amazing! Think about this; the disciple John was on the mount with Peter and James, when Jesus was transfigured right in front of them, and Jesus' face and clothing shone like the sun! They had never seen anything like that before; they were in awe at this glorified presence they were experiencing.

Think about this next example for a moment.

John was the disciple whom Jesus loved. John was always reclining on Jesus' bosom and because of that closeness, received revelation that none of the others received. He *knew* Jesus like no one else.

Yet in Rev. 1:17, when this same disciple, John the beloved, saw the glorified Jesus, he was so overwhelmed at *this* Presence that he fell at His feet as a dead man.

Do you know what that means? That means he encountered *this* version of Jesus, and what he experienced was so far beyond his ability to comprehend Him, that his mind shut down, and he lost consciousness. He fainted. Imagine that! The man who knew Jesus more intimately than any of the other disciples, who walked with Him and talked to Him, and saw Him transfigured in glory, was totally overwhelmed when encountering the glorified Christ. He encountered a different *type* of His presence!

Genesis to Revelation speaks of God's presence in human history. In the Old Testament, the most common Hebrew term for presence is 'panim', translated as "face", implying a close and personal encounter with the Lord. The new testament Greek word 'prosopon' carries the same implication, while the Greek word 'enopion' also appears, showing intimacy.

This is the type of His presence (Panim, or prosopon) you can experience through your expression of true worship! It is the closeness of a face-to-face encounter with God.

While He already knows you completely, a gaze on your part into the Glory of God, even for a moment, has life-altering consequences. This is the time where He is revealing Himself to you, where He's loving on you, and when you commune together.

This is the place of intimacy to which true worship can take you.

Sometimes, there are manifestations with weeping and wailing, while at other times you are prostrated in anguish and can't get off the floor, or quietly kneeling down in thoughtful admiration with tears streaming down your face as you contemplate and *experience* His Goodness.

There are multitudes of physical ways you manifest an encounter with God during these times. The manifestation is not the important thing. You are communing with Almighty God! And there's nothing else like it in the universe. You need to cultivate the desire to enter into *this* type of His intimate presence!

True worship is the vehicle that takes you there.

Why Should You Seek God's Presence?

Why seek God's Presence? I would like to look at some of the Bible verses that tell you exactly what He does, and what He brings with Him when you seek and find Him.

And while I know of the blessings, and His goodness, and how He provides for all of your needs, and moves your enemies out of your way, and how powerful all those are, nothing comes close to comparing with the peace and joy and overwhelming rest that comes with communion with Him.

I don't believe you should be seeking God's presence for what you can get from Him. I don't believe in seeking Him for the *stuff* He gives. In other words, as stated earlier, you should be seeking Him for His face and not for His hands. Yes, He gives! And gives bountifully! But I also believe the more you enter into His presence, the more you love and enjoy the experience, and the desire for the things He gives fades into obscurity.

The Bible is clear that the most important thing to God is finding those people who seek to be with Him. He knows that once you find Him, your life will radically change for the better.

You're told in Ps 53:2 that God is looking down from Heaven for those who are seeking Him.

> *And Heb 11:6 says, "God is a rewarder of those who diligently seek him."*

By the way, 'diligently' doesn't mean, just once, or every blue moon or when the mood strikes you exactly right! It implies a constant and consistent effort, a pressing and pushing toward a goal even if opposition stands in the way. God rewards those who seek Him this way, diligently.

Once you learn that true worship is exactly this—pouring out your heart in adoration, diligently or truly, seeking God with all your heart, all your soul, all your strength, and all your mind—you see why God desires this type of worship. He's been seeking it all along.

Reviewing the Old Testament Scriptures, especially in Psalms, it appears that for a long time God has been seeking, endeavoring, and bending His efforts toward trying to find that person whose sole desire would be to seek after Him. Our verse in John 4:23-24, therefore, is simply another confirmation of a powerful concept found throughout Scripture of God's desire to commune with man.

God *has* been seeking you! And He wants you to seek Him! It's consistently the same thing throughout the ages; He desires a heart totally focused upon and seeking Him. Then when He finds that one, He rewards them. How does He reward them?

> *James 4:8 says, "Draw nigh (near) to God, and he will draw nigh to you..."*

That's the reward! It's Him!

You draw near, and He comes near to you. It's reciprocal; He's the blessing. You find *Him*! And in finding Him, you also reap the benefits that come with Him entering into your presence.

This is what you were made for. We were made to worship Him both individually and collectively. We are supposed to have true worship services every time we come together. Then we're supposed to continue seeking and worshiping Him when we return home so we can experience Him in new and exciting ways. Then when we come back together, each person has a new word of revelation, a new song, a new experience to share with the community of believers so we can encourage each other.

That's how iron sharpens iron.

All this can happen and build up the entire body of believers when you diligently seek after God with all your heart. Which is exactly what happens when you worship.

Here are just a few of the benefits you attain from *finding* Him:

> *Ps 16:11, "You will show me the path of life; In Your presence is fullness of joy; At Your right hand are pleasures forevermore."*
>
> *Ex 33:14, And He said, "My Presence will go with you, and I will give you rest."*
>
> *Ps 34:10, "...But those who seek the Lord shall not lack any good thing."*
>
> *Ps 119:2. "Blessed are those who keep His testimonies, who seek Him with the whole heart"*

The Psalms are filled with verses stressing the importance of seeking God.

> *Psalms 27:4 "One thing have I desired of the Lord, that I will seek after; That I may dwell in the house of the Lord all the days of my life, To behold the beauty of the Lord, and to inquire in his temple."*
>
> *Psalms 27:8 "When thou said, Seek ye my face; my heart said unto thee, Thy face, Lord, will I seek."*
>
> *Psalms 105:4 "Seek the Lord, and his strength: Seek his face evermore."*

Deuteronomy 4:29 gives you the ultimate promise. It says,

> *"If you seek the Lord with all of your heart and soul, you will find Him."*

To seek God with all your heart and soul is synonymous with the condition of true worship in John 4:23-24. Multiple promises come together when this takes place. When you diligently seek Him—true worship—He comes into your presence to reward you. And the reward is Himself, a deeper intimacy with Him than you had previously. When you seek Him with all your heart and soul—true worship again—you find Him!

It all speaks to the incredible connectivity of Scripture.

You worship Him in the way He prescribes, and you are ushered into the most Holy Place to encounter His presence and receive blessings including peace, rest, unspeakable joy, and you never lack any good thing.

The concept of seeking God with all your heart and soul and mind and strength has been what God has been seeking since the beginning of man's existence. When He finds it, He finds a heart reaching out for more of Him, and as He rewards your search, *you* find a new intimate communion with Him.

How to Experience God's Presence: A Desperate Heart

God wants and craves your heart.

"The heart is the one thing God wants from us, but it's the one thing He will not take. It has to be given." M. Heiman

When you become desperate, you are ushered to the end of yourself, the end of your strength, the end of your pride, the end of your self-sufficiency and the end of all that you know to do. It's at *that* point, that the only thing left to do is to cry out to God to come and deliver you!

This kind of desperation seems to only come from focused desire. You've got to want it.

Have you ever been on an athletic team for your high school or college?

I played football, and before the regular season they had what was called 'training camp'. It was a time where we totally dedicated ourselves to the game. Usually, it was ninety-something degrees, and we had on all our pads and equipment, the practices were two hours each, and by the third session of the day, we were beyond weary! We were worn out. Our muscles were strained to the limits, yet the coaches kept pushing for more. They yelled louder and more vigorously as the final practice of the day came to an end, because they knew we were physically at our limits and had to keep pushing us to give more.

One of the main things they would say as they got into our faces, held onto our facemasks, yanking them from side to side, and yelling at the top of their lungs, was, "Do you really want it? Then you've got to give it all you have! Now is the time when everyone else quits! You're not a quitter! You've got to want it more than anything else in the world! Now, run the play again! We're not leaving here until you get it right!"

Something about that time of focused determination enabled us to push past our limits and strive for the goal of running the perfect play. It created a focused desperation within us.

Many times, I've used similar life experiences to gain the proper perspective which helps me press through to get into God's Presence. All the adversity I may be feeling at a particular time, all the distractions coming from every direction, all the times my own fleshly nature simply says, "I don't want to", are viewed as roadblocks attempting to keep me from Him.

So, just as on that football field, I have to push harder. I can't give up and walk away saying, I'll come back later. No! I need Him now! I need His presence more than life. Those roadblocks *must* be removed. And if they're not removed, I'm busting through them! But I'm not leaving until I break through to His presence!"

This is where a focused determination, formed from a desperate heart helps me press forward and destroy every obstacle standing between me and my Lord. I'm forcing all my mind to focus *only* on Him, all my heart to ponder and melt from His goodness, and all my will is commanding every faculty that I have to submit.

We're back to the place of 'in spirit' again. That place we spoke about earlier when that part of us that thinks, wills, feels, and decides takes control. I 'will' myself to get close to God, and any obstacle standing in my way only serves to fuel the desperation of my heart which presses through until I finally rest in God's presence.

Now please understand, I'm not talking about 'works' here.

God already loves us more than we could possibly comprehend. And when He gave Jesus to be a sacrifice for us, He gave His everything to show us that love. We couldn't possibly do anything to earn or deserve more of what He's already given! He *desires* to show

Himself and grow closer in intimacy to us, so we're not talking about working to get into His presence.

But there are hinderances we have that limit our interactions with Him. There are obstacles of the fleshly nature, the carnal mind, worldly distractions, etc…that must be overcome before we can enjoy intimate fellowship with Him.

That's the 'work' we're referring to here.

The disposition of the heart must be carefully guarded, and the distractions of the mind must be corralled until we have a concentrated focus upon Him and Him alone!

Do you feel the desperate need to get into God's intimate presence?

What's hindering you from seeing your lack and His all-sufficiency?

Sometimes, we're just too comfortable with our lives to want to change and move closer into the relationship with God. *Life is good. I have a good paying job. My family has good health. I'm having fun times with my friends. Why do I need to change anything?*

In fact, many times, it takes adverse situations in life that make us uncomfortable before we see the need to ask God for anything. That's just our nature.

We need to work toward cultivating a desperate heart for God and a longing to get into His presence.

Understanding that there's more to be experienced in Him is one way to begin cultivating that heart. And as we turn ourselves towards Him in humble submission, we'll find that He comes and softly communes with us. And through the wonderful experience of His intimate presence, our hearts are set aflame, and we long, desperately, for more.

Old Testament Desperation

"O God, You are my God; Early will I seek You; My soul thirsts for You; My flesh longs for You In a dry and thirsty land Where there is no water." Psalm 63:1.

"As the deer pants for the water brooks, so pants my soul for You, O God. 2 My soul thirsts for God, for the living God. When shall I come and appear before God?" Psalm 42:1,2.

"My soul longs, yes, even faints for the courts of the Lord; my heart and my flesh cry out for the living God." Psalm 84:2.

These are not people seeking God for the first time—these are children seeking *more* of Him. These verses do more than show Old Testament writers who were desperate for God—they show men who were desperate for *more* of God.

Hezekiah's Life Extended

2 Kings 20:1-6: "In those days Hezekiah was sick and near death. And Isaiah the prophet, the son of Amoz, went to him and said to him, "Thus says the Lord: 'Set your house in order, for you shall die, and not live.'" 2 Then he turned his face toward the wall, and prayed to the Lord, saying, 3 "Remember now, O Lord, I pray, how I have walked before You in truth and with a loyal heart, and have done what was good in Your sight." <u>And Hezekiah wept bitterly.</u> 4 And it happened, before Isaiah had gone out into the middle court, that the word of the Lord came to him, saying, 5 "Return and tell Hezekiah the leader

> *of My people, 'Thus says the Lord, the God of David your father: "I have heard your prayer, I have seen your tears; surely I will heal you. On the third day you shall go up to the house of the Lord. 6 And I will add to your days fifteen years. I will deliver you and this city from the hand of the king of Assyria; and I will defend this city for My own sake, and for the sake of My servant David."*

This is amazing!

God had determined that it was time for Hezekiah to die. But Hezekiah, in his desperation, cried out to the Lord, and weeping bitterly, reminded the Lord that he had tried to serve Him and do what was right in God's eyes. Because of Hezekiah's heart, God was moved to change His mind!

Before Isaiah even got through the court of the house, God told him to turn around and go back. His words were, "I have heard your prayer, I have seen your tears: surely I will heal you."

This speaks of *nothing* but the heart of Hezekiah that God was looking at. His prayers and his tears revealed what was in his heart. Desperation brought him to the end of himself and he cried out to God, and that was enough to change God's mind, and God added fifteen years to his life! Then, as if that wasn't enough, He said he would deliver Hezekiah and the entire city from the Assyrians. Hezekiah's heart cry of desperation not only benefitted him but overflowed to produce deliverance for the entire city!

New Testament: Two (Desperate) Blind Men

> <u>Matthew 20:29-34</u>: *"And as they departed from Jericho, a great multitude followed him. And, behold, two blind men sitting by the wayside, when*

> *they heard that Jesus passed by, cried out, saying, Have mercy on us, O Lord, thou Son of David. And the multitude rebuked them, because they should hold their peace: but they cried the more, saying, Have mercy on us, O Lord, thou Son of David. And Jesus stood still, and called them, and said, What will ye that I shall do unto you? They say unto him, Lord, that our eyes may be opened. So, Jesus had compassion on them, and touched their eyes: and immediately their eyes received sight, and they followed him."*

The whole crowd tried to shut them up, but what did they do? They screamed louder! They *knew* the One who could heal their blindness was passing by, and they had *one shot* to get His attention!

That's desperation!

This is how *you* need to be.

Do you believe that God can help you, no matter what the problem is?

Don't let *anything* stop you from getting ahold of the One who can change your situation.

God looks at your heart! And a heart that's desperate is a heart willing to give its all for Him! A desperate heart is a heart of worship; it's down low and humbled, surrendered and submitted, longing in faith for the One who can come and solve their desperate dilemma.

Are You Desperate for More of God?

The New Testament teaches that *'where your treasure is, there will your heart be also.'*

If your treasure is really in heaven, your heart will reside there also, and it will be of absolutely no consequence if you are required to use all your earthly treasures to obtain it.

'American Christians live in the most prosperous nation in world history and the one in which it costs the *least* to be a Christian.

'This environment of comfort breeds the exact opposite of desperation and can be deadly to faith, as it allows false faith to masquerade as real. Comfort can drain our zeal and energy, our focus and willingness to risk for the Lord, because it's not based upon trusting *Him* for all our needs. It trusts only in our own strength, our own wisdom, our financial situation, etc… to keep us living in the ease we've become accustomed to.

'Comfort doesn't come to us at gunpoint or with the threat of bodily harm! It comes with a pillow and a promise of ease for us and our children. The former makes us desperate for God. The latter robs our sense of desperation, and therefore drains us of our faith *in* God!

'It's this lack of a sense of desperation for God that is so deadly! If we don't feel desperate for God, we will not cry out to Him!' What has happened to our hearts when we cannot go to God in desperate prayer, and cry out for those loved ones who are dying and on their way to hell?

'Love for this present world sets in subtly, like a spiritual leprosy, damaging spiritual nerve endings so that we don't feel the erosion and decay happening until it's too late!'

This is going to sound strange, but 'we need to fast and pray for God to deliver us from the disease of prosperity and comfort!'

I'm not advocating that prosperity in and of itself is your main issue. It's not. It's always the condition of the heart that is of primary concern. But too many in the Church who were blessed with financial prosperity have allowed it to control their hearts instead of using it as a means through which they can bless and help others. We've used our blessings to heap more material goods upon ourselves which lead to a more comfortable lifestyle which in turn prevents us from considering that we have more need for God!

God is Who we need! We need *Him*!

You can discipline yourself in various ways. It can happen, but it's difficult to manufacture desperation while living in comfort. You can have a renewed focus and determination to seek Him, knowing by faith that He will come to your side and bless you with His presence. You can use what you've learned 'in spirit', and place that part of you that thinks, feels, wills, and decides down before the Lord, making the willful decision to surrender all you have and all you are to Him. You can ask Him for His assistance. He loves to answer His children, especially in response to their desire to have more of Him.

He *will* help you!

God can change your heart or alter your circumstances to make you desperate for Him.

Please then, fervently and passionately seek the Lord's Presence with everything you have within you, and with all of your faculties. It doesn't matter whether you come with singing, or dancing, in thanksgiving, or praise, or move directly into worship. What truly matters is the condition of your heart while approaching His throne.

If your heart has been made low, and humbled, and surrendered, and submitted to the Lord, I promise He will do the rest and usher you into a new level of intimacy with Him.

This is the place of true worship! The Secret Place. You will be at His feet. And you will be in His presence, where there is joy unspeakable, and full of glory.

CHAPTER TWELVE

A DESPERATE WOMAN

We've already discussed Mary's alabaster box of precious ointment. But she's not our only example. In the New Testament, you see it every time you see people with the condition of the heart, or assuming the physical position of the body.

> *Mark 5:25-34: "And a certain woman, which had an issue of blood twelve years, and had suffered many things of many physicians, and had spent all that she had, and was nothing bettered, but rather grew worse, When she had heard of Jesus, came in the press behind, and touched his garment. For she said, If I may touch but his clothes, I shall be whole. And straightway the fountain of her blood was dried up; and she felt in her body that she was healed of that plague. And Jesus, immediately knowing in himself that virtue had gone out of him, turned him about in the press, and said, "Who touched my clothes?" And his disciples said unto him, "Thou seest the multitude thronging thee, and sayest thou, Who touched me?" And he looked round about to see her that had done this thing. But the woman fearing and trembling, knowing what was done in her, came and fell down*

> *before him, and told him all the truth. And he said unto her, "Daughter, thy faith hath made thee whole; go in peace and be whole of thy plague."*

Out of desperation, this woman traveled to seek out the man who, just by the touch of his clothes, could heal the sick and diseased. All she had was her faith in Jesus! She had *no other choice*! All the doctors of the day had failed. All of her money was gone. If Jesus wouldn't heal her, all her hope would be lost.

It was an incredible mission of desperation and faith fueled by an incurable blood disorder that made her ceremonially unclean (according to Mosaic Law) and socially unacceptable. She wasn't even allowed to be there!

In those days, to prevent the inadvertent touching of those that were ceremonially clean with those who were unclean, the diseased person would have to walk the streets yelling, "Unclean!" And people would get out of their way. No one wanted to come into contact with someone unclean.

But what did she do? The Bible says that she,

> *"...came in the press behind and touched his garment."*

There was a large crowd of people gathered around and walking with Jesus. She never yelled that she was unclean but instead she came up from behind Him to touch Him.

Mark says 'touch His clothes', but Matthew tells *where* she touched Him.

It was on the hem of His garment. Where is the hem of His garment located? There are many that believe the hem was at the bottom portion of His robe, where His feet and sandals contacted the dirt. Others say it was located around the four corners of the prayer shawl, which extended in most cases down to the thigh.

She had to be down on her knees, creeping through the crowd to touch Him if the hem was down by His feet. This seems likely since she had this issue of blood for a long time and would have been known by the people thronging around Jesus. She had to be hidden or disguised, or both!

In faith and desperation, she reached out for a miracle to relieve her physical and emotional suffering, and it caught the attention of Jesus. As soon as she touched the Master's garment, she was restored! Jesus spoke to her using the word 'daughter' as a term of endearment. It indicated that she was no longer an outsider, but rather an accepted family member. Her uncleanness had been cured.

You see the condition of her heart was that of desperation. She *had* to get to Jesus! She had no other choice! She had to disregard what others would think, what trouble she would be in if she were discovered. She had to will herself to approach Jesus in spite of all the opposition. Nothing was going to get in her way.

You see desperation! And in seeing her desperation, you see the condition of her heart!

You see faith! She said, "If I could just touch His clothes, I will be made whole!" She trusted wholeheartedly in His ability to heal her. You can, quite possibly, see the position of her body was down low and kneeling or crouching to touch the hem of His garment at His feet.

You see all the elements of true worship; her heart, her body, her faith, and that it was done publicly.

When discovered, she walks to Him, and falls down, pouring out her heart or telling Him all the truth! Even if the position hadn't been there as she touched Him, it was now. These are all characteristics of worship taking place!

And you see that each time worship is given, the people exhibiting it receive what they came to Jesus for.

Here's a neat project to take away from this lesson.

Go throughout the Gospels and write down every time someone is exhibiting the heart condition of a worshiper or puts themselves down into a low bodily position to approach Jesus.

Here are a few of the many examples in the New Testament gospels: Mary and Martha, anyone at His feet; prostrated before Him or kneeling…

It's an intriguing study!

Each example will show the person giving Him the worship He desires, receiving from Him what they came for. Please understand, true worship is not a formula to make God do whatever you want Him to do. God is not your spiritual Santa Claus! You worship Him with all of your heart, and soul, and strength, because you love Him. Period. Whatever benefits you gain, are simply the wonderful overflowing side effects of living this life of loving Him, which leads to your obedience.

From God's perspective, true worship *is* what He's looking for, seeking, and actively bending His efforts toward trying to find. When He finally apprehends that which His heart's been endeavoring to find, He speedily comes to the side of His child in response to their needs.

What's *your* need?

Do you need forgiveness from sin? Is there emotional pain you want Him to relieve? How about unanswered questions, painful circumstances, or a desperation to be in His presence?

It doesn't matter what the need comprises.

The God of the universe who called all things into existence with a word from His mouth, will come near and hold you! And in holding you, you will discover that there's no problem too large for Him. He parted the Red Sea with a blast from His nostrils. So, do you really think your issue is beyond His ability?

Oh, ye of little faith.

Draw close and worship Him and watch Him come to your aid!

CHAPTER THIRTEEN

A WORSHIP EXPERIENCE

A few of my brothers in Christ and I, who had been raised up and discipled by an incredible man of God to understand and give God true worship, felt God was leading us to go to a large, three-to-four-thousand member church that was several hours drive from where we lived at the time.

We piled into a van and cars and drove there one Sunday morning for service.

It was a Palm Sunday.

It was an exciting time for us as a group. We were getting accustomed to hearing from the Lord and moving out in the direction He would lead us, and because of our obedience and willingness to give God true worship, He allowed us to be in the center of various experiences where we saw God move powerfully in the lives of others.

This is one of those experiences.

We arrived a little early and sat together in a row in the pew, waiting for the service to begin.

It wasn't long after the song service started, and praises started being proclaimed throughout the church, that I began to feel a weight on my shoulders. The only way that I can describe it is that I just felt heavy! As if I was being weighted down with a heavy vest, as if someone pushed in a downward direction on my shoulders. Within moments, the heaviness, though it stayed upon my shoulders, extended to my heart, and I felt the urge to cry!

It was almost as if someone very close to me was dying.

Was it my Mother? No, it wasn't that. My brother or sister? No, I wasn't feeling this heart pain for either of them. I searched my heart, asking God to help me. What is it, Lord? What is this continually growing agony wrenching through my chest?

My children? Oh, dear Lord, that's it! It felt as if my children were dying!

How can one describe how a parent feels when their child is dying?

Your chest sustains an unbearable weight, and your heart feels as though it may burst from the anguish of the soul! It's an unquenchable pain! Unplumbed depths of sorrow which you think may swallow you up, and from which it seems you may never return.

This was the inner turmoil thrust upon me, and there was nothing I could do to avoid or stop it.

It quickly became overwhelming.

All I could do was sit in the pew and weep over a pain I hadn't yet fully perceived the purpose of, for a child genuinely loved, to whom I never recognized my parenthood.

It all *sounds* of confusion, but the Bible tells us that God is not the author of confusion. So, I croaked out a plea to God for understanding of what I was experiencing. And immediately He answered as a thought dawned upon my troubled mind that God was enjoining my heart to His!

He was allowing me to feel a miniscule amount of what He feels for His people.

It was devastating.

The feeling I had of *my* children dying, weighing down my heart, wasn't really about *my* children, but His. It was *His* pain for *His* children, and *His* longing to come into their midst and heal them of everything that ailed them, that I was experiencing! It was not only His pain, but also His desire to rush to the aid of His children, sweeping over me in a swell of emotion. Who knew God would feel this way? And with such depth as to make me cringe in anguish as if I would burst at the seams if this weight were not lifted!

I instinctively knew that this was but an *iota* of what God felt! I knew that what was but a miniscule portion of what God feels for us, would *literally* make me pass into unconsciousness if the intensity of this burden wasn't soon lifted. As I sat in the pew, hunched over my knees, I looked down the row at my brothers in Christ that had accompanied me, and they were hunched over too, arms folded across their stomachs as if in pain as well! Right next to me, one of them had tears streaming down his face.

We *all* were experiencing the same thing! God was pouring out His heart, allowing us to feel what He feels, and we were literally at the point of swooning in turmoil.

It took everything within me to keep the guttural wrenching of my soul to quiet moans and groans while the song service went on. And from the faces drenched in tears and disfigured in agony, I knew each one of the men accompanying me was having the same experience.

Many leading pastors that we've since spoken to have said that God doesn't do this, or God doesn't work this way. He would never put pain or anguish on you in the manner that I have described.

But the Word of God says differently, as we've seen in the lives of various apostles, prophets and men and women of God!

Back at the church, I'm not sure how long the inner anguish lasted, but it continued to intensify within my bowels until I felt I was going to burst. I *had* to get released from this agony! But what could I do?

At that moment, one of the guys next to me stood up, loudly saying over the music of the song service, "I can't take it anymore!"

and he quickly stepped by me and headed down the aisle toward the altar!

Since I was at the same spiritual, mental, and emotional place, desperately needing release, I followed closely behind him groaning in wrenching inner turmoil as I walked. It wasn't until we arrived at the altar that I realized every one of the guys had jumped up to follow. At once, we had formed a procession of tearful men streaming down the aisle to the front of the church! We fell on our faces, prostrated ourselves on the altar, and began pouring out our hearts with weeping and wailing to God for the anguish that we felt inside. The intensity of our internal turmoil was only matched by the screams and wails of weeping and moaning that ushered forth from each one of us. It became so loud, that it seemed to overwhelm the music of the service, until at last, the music stopped as the pastor stepped to the podium.

For a few moments, everything was quiet in the church, the music, the people, except for the screaming, wailing cries of those of us lying prostrate at the altar. From my perspective on the floor, the roar was deafening!

(This next portion was told to us by the pastor who invited us back into his office after the service had ended. I have combined the pastor's words with what I was experiencing to give you a more full description of what was taking place.)

We continued on the floor weeping, wailing, and groaning as the pastor started speaking.

"I was on the plane coming home," he said, "when the Lord told me that He was sending men to our church this morning. He showed me men on their knees and on their faces weeping and crying in pain. I asked the Lord, 'What did they do, Lord? Are they in sin? What should I do? How do I handle this?'

"This is what the Lord answered. 'These men are not in sin, neither are they crying out for themselves, but for you and for this house. In this time, I will visit you.'"

Someone screamed, then various cries sounded from throughout the church as people began individually experiencing powerful manifestations of the Presence of God within their midst.

The pastor continued, "In this time, I will heal and deliver. Advanced stages of AIDS and cancer will be no more. Deliverance from every kind of spiritual darkness. I will set My people free."

Within moments, the atmosphere grew thick and heavy with God's presence! And from the guttural yelling and screaming that ushered forth from those in the congregation, it seemed as if an unseen hand was touching the deepest of hurts, and opening doors of anguish that had long since been closed and locked.

I could actually feel the floor of the church rumble, as people started running down the aisles and arrived at the altar right by our sides, where they too fell down crying and weeping.

The pastor continued in his own words. "I looked for the men in the early service this morning and no one was here." (We arrived at the 11 a.m. service. Apparently, they had had an early service at 9 a.m. too.)

The pastor continued, "I thought maybe I was wrong in what I thought I heard from God, but now I see it clearly. Today is the day of God's visitation."

I opened my eyes slightly to look through my tears. My vision was blurred, my eyes red and swollen from all the crying. Everything seemed foggy, and although I saw a multitude of people standing, kneeling, and lying on the floor of the altar with us, arms raised, crying, and wailing to God, I closed my eyes again to shut them all out. I didn't want distractions. This was *my* time with the Lord! My time to give my all to Him, and distractions only served the flesh. My brothers and I continued to weep and wail loudly as wave upon wave of God's presence flowed over us.

How does one describe the introduction of that which is eternal into the realm of we who are merely mortal?

In a word, overwhelming. In every way, shape, and form! It was simply overwhelming!

I lay on the floor of the altar, cringing as if I was actually having the contractions of a woman in childbirth! My midsection contracted over and over each time another wave of the Master swept through me. It was as if I was having a spiritual baby. I was in travail! The relaxing time between contractions wasn't empty of His presence but charged with a different type of manifestation as He poured out His love upon me! It was all I could do to maintain who I was in that time! It was as if who I really was inside, the part of me that's just like Him, was so entwined and entangled and one with God, that I felt as if I may burst!

God's desires became my desires, and I knew, as I did in the beginning, that His children were dying, and He was longing to commune with and heal them. The agony of the anguish was now gone.

God had arrived in our midst! And He knew that when He arrived, He would set all things in place, healing and delivering His children. Though my travail was over, waves of adoration and love from Him to us, and from us to Him, remained to sweep over us. We were truly one with our Creator. It was a glorious time in God's presence.

The pastor later told us that the glory of God had formed as a fog or mist and started descending in the church.

That was what I saw when I opened my eyes! It wasn't that my eyes had been blurred from crying, and they definitely had been that. But I was *actually seeing* the manifested Glory of God in the form of a fog or mist!

I'm not sure how long the cries and wails continued. The pastor knew God was visiting their church that morning, and he let Him continue for as long as He wanted.

We heard otherworldly screams from several places in the church as demons were shrieking out, being ejected from people. All this took place without one person laying hands upon another. God was in the place, and when that which is Perfect is come, that which is in part – which is *any* ministry on our part – is done away!

God ministered to each person in ways we could never have imagined they required, and on a level that *no* man has access to. It was amazing!

I tell that story *not* because I want each of you to know what we did. But because what I've been describing, and the incredible manifestation that followed, came from giving God true worship.

This is just one example *of many* of what God *can* and *will* do when you give Him what He's looking for.

An entire church was transformed in that brief encounter with God.

I'm not special! Neither are the men that were with me on that day. Well, we're all special in the sight of God; however, since God is not a respecter of persons, He will do for you all that He has done for me and perhaps more. It's up to *you* to begin to long for His presence and give Him what *He's* looking for.

Weeks later, we received confirmation of what God did in the people of that church on that Palm Sunday morning. They came to church with doctors' exams, and clean bills of health from their physicians stating that their doctors had no medical explanation for what happened in the person. Each one had been totally healed!

This is what can happen when God shows up in your midst.

He's longing to do the same for you!

But again, it all starts with giving Him what He's been looking for. He will come into your midst and give you the gift of Himself. And when you have Him, whatever it is that you need in that moment, He's there to supply.

CHAPTER FOURTEEN

WORSHIP AND FAITH

Faith is crucial to the Christian life. It's foundational.

Hebrews 11:1 says, "Now faith is the substance of things hoped for, the evidence of things not seen."

The New Testament word for faith is the Greek word pistis, (pronounced pis-tis), and means, assurance, belief, confidence, conviction, faith, fidelity, persuasion, reliance upon God and upon his Word, and trust.

It is this assurance, belief, confidence, trust, and reliance upon God and upon His Word that forms the substance of things hoped for, the evidence of things not seen.

The Greek word for substance means foundation, or substructure.

What this verse is saying is that it is faith, or your belief, or your trust in and reliance upon God that forms the substructure, or foundation for all the things that you hope for, or confidently expect to receive from God, but the evidence or proof of those things remains unseen or invisible.

As Christians, you should be trusting, or put another way, placing faith in God for everything that you need. He is the one who

WORSHIP AND FAITH

has been providing for you, keeping you safe and secure, and bringing you through the situations in life that otherwise would have caused you harm.

But faith is not limited to be toward God.

All of us apply faith to many things. In fact, every one of us, every day, places faith in objects!

You walk over to a chair or a couch and plop yourself down without ever checking the strength or stability of that piece of furniture! You simply *know* that it supported you before, and you have the confident expectation that it will support you again. That's trusting in what you confidently expect, without really having any evidence that what you want will actually take place. That's placing faith in an object.

It is exactly the same with God! Once you realize that He has been with you your entire life, protecting you, holding you, stabilizing situations, preventing you from bodily harm, and loving you through all the changes in your life, your perspective changes. You begin to trust Him more. You learn to fully plop yourself down into His hand, having a strong belief that since He's been there for you before, you can confidently expect Him to be there for you again. That's faith in God!

Faith is so fundamental to the Christian walk and so powerful for how you should live, that Scripture says when He comes back, He'll be looking for faith so He can take you home.

Faith is powerful!

So, when Jesus was describing what the Father was seeking after, looking for, actively bending His efforts toward trying to find in our Bible verse John 4:23-24, why didn't He say the Father is actively seeking a man of faith? One would think that since faith is *so* integral to the Christian life, He would be seeking that!

In our previous chapter, you have seen and studied the power of thanksgiving and praise, and how they can elevate your heart to a narrow focus upon God and bring you to a place where God is enthroned upon the celebratory glory you ascribe to Him.

Praise is powerful!

But why isn't God seeking a man of true and constant praise?

What about money?

I've heard so many Christians say that God can't do anything through the Church or any other organization without money. If that's true, doesn't God need your money to do the good works Scriptures speak of?

Why not seek a true tither? One who tithes constantly and consistently so God can get accomplished what He wants to get done in the earth.

But from Jesus' own lips, He expresses the fact that the Father is not seeking or endeavoring to find any of those other things. That doesn't mean that they aren't important! Each has its place of prominence within the Christian lifestyle. It is not a question of what has importance, but of what is *most* important to God.

True Worship is the thing Scripture says He's actively looking for. That's incredible in the light of how necessary those other Christian qualities and characteristics are!

But why is true worship what He's looking for?

It's because the particular kind of worship that God desires, encompasses the totality of your being.

Its effects touch everything that you are, and everything that you have. In effect, once He has this kind of worship, He has *all* of you! In fact, I dare say that I don't think I've studied anything else in His Word that compares to it. Nothing else in Scripture requires that you surrender all that you are and all that you have to God before you can partake in it.

Let me explain.

In my opinion, salvation is the most transformational occurrence that takes place in life. When you learn what happened to you at salvation, you will see that it is a miracle beyond miracles! And many

WORSHIP AND FAITH

people—hopefully most—will surrender their lives to Christ in humble submission, allowing Him to take control and guide their decisions from then on.

Salvation is amazing!

That act of total surrender and submission to God (condition) in faith where you leave your old selfish ways behind and press forward (in spirit) into believing in Him as your sole source for everything, makes the process of salvation a type of worshiping God in spirit and in truth!

Yep. When you gave your life to Christ, you also took the first step toward giving God what He had been desiring all along! He wants your all. Isn't that what you give when you commit to Christ?

You ask Him into your life so He can be not only your Savior, but also your Lord. This lordship means that you're fully giving Him control of you, which means you are fully surrendered to Him.

Surrender, submission, down low in heart asking for Him to come into your life whether for the first time, or more intimately—both are at the heart of true worship.

And what happens at salvation after you cry out for Him? He comes into your life and your second state is more intimate than you were before.

What happens when you cry out to Him in worship? He manifests to you in multiple ways, and while you bask in His presence, your state after worshiping Him is more intimate than it was before.

Do you see the connection?

Your experience in salvation was not only meant to do the miraculous and snatch you from the kingdom of darkness and transport you into the Kingdom of God. It was also your blueprint for continuing in intimate communion with God throughout the rest of your life in true worship! They are the same in character.

The attributes of surrender, submission, pleading for Him to come close, a heart overflowing with gratitude, etc... are what identify true worship in the Bible, and once you see these foundational characteristics, you will see them *everywhere* throughout Scripture!

When you see someone in the physical position of being down low, prostrate, at His feet, kneeling, bowing, or crouching, and coming to Christ in faith, trusting, believing, relying upon Him or in the power of His Word, they are candidates for true worship. Additionally, when you read of someone in Scripture with the necessary heart condition for true worship which is also down low, broken, in tears or weeping, in adoration, surrender, submitting the whole of who they are to Christ, these too become candidates for worship if they come in full faith, believing in Him.

The joining assumption would also be that if they are worshipping God in the way He desires, that they are trusting, believing, and placing their fullest confidence in Him as well.

Yes, faith and true worship are inseparably linked.

But it should be noted that this connection is only in one direction.

You can have faith in God and your worship still be untrue.

I believe this is the state of many in the Church in America and perhaps other parts of the world today. There are those who claim Christianity, but who live differently than God desires, those in the flesh, and those living in sin and carnality.

Then there are those who know the meaning of true worship but aren't worshiping Him constantly, faithfully, or sincerely. They all say that they have faith, or trust in God, but in their actions and lifestyle, they don't want to do any more to continue to strengthen that relationship. So, supposedly they have faith, but their worship remains untrue.

As I've said, faith and worship are linked, but only in one direction.

You can have faith in God and not worship Him truly.

But you *cannot* worship God in the true manner that He desires without having faith!

WORSHIP AND FAITH

Faith, being your belief, your trust, your reliance upon God and upon His Word, with true worship being the heart condition of adoration, the deepest reverence, the highest honor you can give to God.

The resulting manifestation exuding from the heart from such an extreme condition of trust and adoration is total surrender and complete submission to the One you have identified as your Source.

It's all about the heart!

It's from the heart that faith flows, and from the heart that worship ensues.

I've said this quote from an incredibly wise friend of mine before, and I'll continue to say it because it's so important for you to understand.

"The heart is the one thing God requires, but it's the one thing He *will not take*. It has to be given." M. Heiman

He was speaking of the heart as the control center of the body. And once that control center is fully submitted to God in faith, all that you are becomes His to do with as He pleases.

True worship flows from and encompasses a heart fully surrendered to God in faith. Although God is earnestly seeking after this condition of heart, He will not forcefully take it. It must be freely given to Him. The worshiper must be fully trusting (placing faith in, or faithing) in Him, knowing that He is, in order to worship Him in this manner.

> *Hebrews 11:6 says, "But without faith it is impossible to please Him: for he that comes to God must believe that He is, and that He is a rewarder of them that diligently seek Him."*

So, you can't come to God unless you believe, or trust, or have confidence in the fact that He is! He's alive and He wants to be in your life! That's faith! You must *believe* that He exists and that He will reward those who diligently seek Him! Remember when we talked about the ties between diligently seeking Him and truly seeking or worshiping Him? Both 'diligently' and 'truly' speak of seeking Him faithfully, constantly, and consistently. Diligently implies a constant effort, even while in the face of adversity or opposition.

It's the same as worshiping in spirit, where we have to press and push, using that part of ourselves that thinks, feels, wills, and decides to move into God's presence.

God is a rewarder of those who worship Him truly and diligently. But as the previous verses in Hebrews state, this person must *first* believe that He is, which means that they come to Him in faith.

For worship to be true, you must first believe that God *is*, and that He is with you! You come to Him in faith and move closer in adoration. True worship *is* diligently seeking Him *in faith*!

Worship, like diligence, requires pressing with *all* your heart, *all* your soul, *all* your mind, and *all* your strength, and in doing so, you are believing or trusting that He is and that He rewards those who seek Him this way. Therefore, worship encompasses all your *faith* as well.

All your faith, all your praise, all your finances, all your emotions, all your heart, all your mind, it's everything you have and everything you are, loving and ministering to Him in the only way *He* prescribes!

This is the connection between Worship and Faith.

And this is the reason God is actively seeking a true worshiper to worship Him. Because faith and worship are inextricably intertwined.

Faith forms the boundaries around which you begin to worship God. And in doing so, you worship Him fully, trusting in Him for more of His presence.

Then worship, and the intimate encounters with God that it presents, begins to encompass and strengthen your faith as you press further into greater intimacy with God.

CHAPTER FIFTEEN

WORSHIP AND BROKENNESS

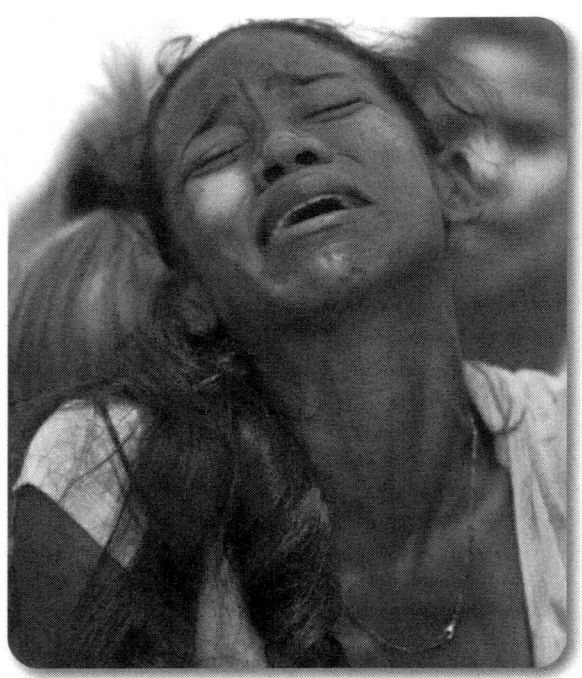

Worship and brokenness are dependent upon each other and as intertwined as two sides of the same coin.

If worship is the death of, or the willful surrender of, all your heart and soul and strength and mind in adoration toward God

TRUE WORSHIP: THE GATEWAY TO INTIMACY WITH GOD

with all that process entails, then brokenness is the vehicle God uses to overcome the obstacles of the flesh and drive you toward *that* submissive end.

Unfortunately, we in the Church have a difficult time with the topic of brokenness because most really don't understand what it means.

So, let's look at it. What does it mean to be broken?

The world's definition of broken is splintered, forcibly fractured, violated, no good, weak, tamed, or subdued. These are not all the words in the definition, but you get the idea! It's *definitely* not a good thing!

Unfortunately, the Church has absorbed the world's definition and added in some of our own insights, which resulted in a worldly understanding of brokenness that we then apply to spiritual principles.

Let's say you go to the store to make a purchase, but when you return, you discover that the item you just purchased is broken. You say these are damaged goods, and you take it back, or throw it away.

From *that* perspective, broken is a word and a concept that stands for something that doesn't work properly, something that's in pieces. Useless. This is how we react to broken things, therefore the definition applied to it seems to make sense.

When you arrive at church and hear the preacher say that you were once broken from sin, but Jesus came and now you are made whole again, there *is* truth to it, so it makes sense to you.

We acknowledge *the idea* of brokenness when we're hurting from the storms of life that come to each one of us. You say, "I feel so broken", as you look for help or prayer from others so God can give you strength to make you whole again. As those storms rage on, you continue to apply the world's definition to your situation, thinking you've done something wrong, that God is angry with you, or you feel broken in pieces and useless. Some even go so far as to think so profoundly of their worthlessness that they feel they ought to be discarded.

Through it all, the idea of 'brokenness' takes on a sinister character that you do everything in your power to avoid.

I totally understand. With those preconceived notions of the topic, I'd try to avoid it too!

Thankfully, God looks at life, and you, a lot differently.

True biblical brokenness is not opposed to your wholeness in Him. On the contrary, it is *through* brokenness that you are exposed to an entirely different kind of strength, which in turn makes you truly whole.

Brokenness is actually a part of the process of sanctification.

Sanctification is being separated from the profane things, or from the world, and separated unto God or for His purposes. Many books have been written about what sanctification is as a theological topic. And various theories have been forwarded as to the various methods by which it can be accomplished in the believer.

Brokenness is one of those powerful methods of *how* sanctification takes place.

It is how God accomplishes His changes, and breaks you away from who you were, to who you will be, which is conformed into the image of Christ. I would never be so bold as to say it's the *only* way God separates you *from* the profane things of the world and separates you *unto* Himself, but it's definitely one of the major avenues He uses.

Here's how brokenness works.

We all were, "…born in sin and shaped in iniquity". We were born opposed to God. After coming to Christ, we don't lose that opposing nature. I know many theologians say we do, but we feel its influence every day! That's why Paul exclaimed, "I die daily!" Because it's a constant battle, and it's still with us. Always attempting to move us toward carnality and away from holiness.

This nature *must* be put down, crucified, made to die, and confronted until the sacrifice stops kicking on the altar!

Notice how Paul described the war within himself in Romans 7:18-24 (ESV).

> *"For I know that nothing good dwells in me, that is, in my flesh. For I have the desire to do what is right, but not the ability to carry it out.* [19] *For I do not do the good I want, but the evil I do not want is what I keep on doing.* [20] *Now if I do what I do not want, it is no longer I who do it, but sin that dwells within me.*
>
> [21] *So I find it to be a law that when I want to do right, evil lies close at hand.* [22] *For I delight in the law of God, in my inner being,* [23] *but I see in my members another law waging war against the law of my mind and making me captive to the law of sin that dwells in my members.* [24] *Wretched man that I am! Who will deliver me from this body of death?"*

You can almost hear the anguish in his writing!

The things he *wants* to do, he *can't* because of this struggle within, and the things he wants to avoid, those things he keeps on doing. In desperation, he seems to loudly cry out, "Oh wretched man that I am! Who will deliver me from this body of death?"

He longed for the spiritual life within him to take control, but the flesh that still dominated him at that time fought for supremacy. This is the same war that is going on within our members as well!

It's good to know that we, like Paul, *can* have the victory over the fleshly nature. Part of that victory comes through renewing your minds to the Word of God, another portion through God's process of brokenness, and another when you learn to die to Self.

This is what brokenness is meant to do. Kill that part of you that is opposed to the things of God, and fights to control you. It's meant to kill the flesh.

It's a means by which your carnal nature is brought into a place of surrender under the control of *your* spirit, which is supposed to be submitted to the dominion of the Holy Spirit.

Look at Jeremiah 18:1-6.

> "The word which came to Jeremiah from the Lord, saying, ² Arise, and go down to the potter's house, and there I will cause thee to hear my words. ³ Then I went down to the potter's house, and behold, he wrought a work on the wheels. ⁴ And the vessel that he made of clay was marred in the hand of the potter: so, he made it again another vessel, as seemed good to the potter to make it. ⁵ Then the word of the Lord came to me, saying, ⁶ O house of Israel, cannot I do with you as this potter? saith the Lord. Behold, as the clay is in the potter's hand, so are ye in mine hand, O house of Israel."

This is an example of God and His people. You belong to Him! You are not your own.

Doesn't the potter have the right to make the clay into whatever pleases Him?

The clay is just a lump in the beginning. But at the Master's touch, the clay begins to take form. He pulls off pieces and discards what is not needed. Forming, shaping, tearing off, and reforming, molding into an image already crystal clear in the potter's mind. Finally, as if all that went before was nothing but a preamble for what awaited, the fully formed item still must be placed in the furnace and heated to expose any remaining flaws within it. Only afterwards is it able to be what the Master intended it to be.

When you come to Christ, you're changed and made new. But you still have old habits and a fleshly nature you must fight against. God brings brokenness events into your life to break the stubbornness of the carnal nature and allow the power of the Spirit to flow outward to the world.

This is God as the potter, doing the molding, the crushing, the wedging and shaping! He's conforming it into an image.

Have you ever stopped to consider what this process feels like for the clay?

You usually don't because clay is an inanimate object, and most people don't identify with non-living objects. But think about it. In God's analogy, what would it feel like to continually be smashed, and shaped, and folded over, and pressed together again and again until that time arrives that the Master knows the clay is ready to be placed upon the wheel and formed into the vessel He requires?

What about when He tears pieces off and discards them?

Here's a question. 'How do you feel when things don't go as planned... when it rains on your parade... when someone says something hurtful... when our world turns upside down through the death of a child...when a spouse leaves...we get turned down for that promotion we deserve - the long and short of it is, it makes us angry! We are devastated, hurt and humiliated!

Perhaps He doesn't *cause* them all, but God *uses* those circumstances along with reproaches, abuse, poverty, loneliness, persecution, distress, seeming failure, disappointments, and the like to rid us of our carnal nature!'

That's God's part! That's Him smashing, forming, wedging, and molding you as clay.

And He is in control of the process at every turn; there is nothing you can do to prevent it.

These things succeed in doing what they were meant to do when they cause you to come to the end of yourself, and let God take control.

This is the process of brokenness.

There is an incredible phrase from writer Elizabeth Eliot that should be taken to heart. "God will not protect you from anything that will make you more like Christ."

That's sobering when you give it some thought.

You are predestined to be conformed to the image of Christ.

This was determined long before the world began and will not change because you don't like the way it feels.

I was like so many Christians that failed to discern the purpose of the circumstances they were going through. I insisted on the devil being the culprit and I thought I was fighting in a spiritual war. All the opposition I faced was the devil working through men, through the environment around me, or through my circumstances.

We stumble and fight because we've been taught that the Lord will not do anything to cause what we perceive to be harm. He's a God of love, and therefore cannot bring hurt into our lives, right?

I understand this thinking! I grew up believing the same things.

In attempting to make the situation better, we quote Bible verses, attempt to engage in spiritual warfare, and pray to bind up the power of the devil who is bringing the pain. These are positive spiritual practices, and no one can fault anyone for attempting them to find relief. 'Most believers think their renewed obedience and prayers will make the clouds go away, the skies turn blue, the sun will shine, their financial problems will disappear, and their nest egg will grow again!' When things don't turn around and become better from your perspective, many times, you give up and think the devil won.

But God gave me a revelation a long time ago that changed *everything* for me.

It was *not* the enemy working in my life.

It was Him. God was doing it.

This *devastated* me.

My entire theology got turned upside down. All my spiritual warfare had been for naught!

It wasn't the devil at all, but God I was fighting against! I was resisting *His* plans to break me to bring me under *His* control. What I *needed* to do was surrender to Him and ask what it was I needed to learn through His process. He was shaping and conforming me to the image of His Son Jesus.

In my cries for help, sometimes God gave me a reprieve, depending upon where I was in His process.

Other times, He didn't.

Is God still good? Absolutely.

In fact, it's was *through* these hardships that He drew me closer to Himself and showed me His Goodness.

The point is, sometimes being conformed hurts.

This process is not from the devil, and not because some evil has been sent against you. It's God doing the molding and forming because it was decreed before the foundations of the world that each person in Christ is predestined to be conformed to His image!

I want you to let something sink in.

This was God doing the molding and shaping. God was doing something that caused hurt.

This may sound foreign to some of you.

We always quote Romans 8, saying,

> *God works all things together for the good of them who love God and are called according to His purpose.*

In this, we say that God *only* makes good things happen for those who love Him.

But technically, that's not what it's saying. He's saying He'll make everything that happens to you eventually work to the good.

By the way, He's working all things together for 'the' good, not for 'my' good as we always misquote it. It's just a small technicality, but it changes your perception immensely.

If you interpret that He's working for 'my' good, you will always assume a positive journey, because it's all about me, and everything He's doing is so I can have the outcome where I come out on top. Working things together for 'the' good, conversely, implies it's actually for the overall good, in other words it's for *His* good, which will be for *your* good *eventually*, but it may not feel like it in the moment. It might not even feel good anytime in the immediate future.

This is a poor analogy, but did you ever get a spanking when you were young?

I did.

Did it feel good in the moment? Of course not! It was meant to be a deterrent to some of the things you may have been doing. But the long-term objective was to work something in you that prevented you from disobedient behavior that would eventually land you in much deeper trouble.

The immediate pain of the spanking was working obedience into you so that you learned not to transgress Mom and Dad's rules anymore. But it also worked something deeper in you. You learned not to disobey the rules because there would be consequences.

Sometimes, painful ones.

In fact, most of the guys I ministered to in prison ministry thought that their lives would be drastically better if they'd had parents who had been active early in their lives and disciplined them when they were young. They would have hated it then, but they felt they would be vastly different individuals now.

God does the same thing when He chastises us, and when He allows brokenness events in your life. He just does it *perfectly*, knowing exactly how the issues He brings into your life will affect you, and how you will respond. He allows and sometimes orchestrates issues for you to navigate, knowing that the outcome will bring a closer, more intimate relationship with Him.

That is the greater good!

For that to be accomplished, He *must* break you.

Listen to this next quote as you read it.

"God loves you way too much to allow you to stay the way you are." Author unknown.

This is brokenness. It is the process of being shaped and conformed until you are fit for the Master's use. It is through this process that you develop the heart of total surrender necessary for true worship.

The Importance of Brokenness

"We know God has the power to save us, we just don't really believe He's better at leading our lives than we are."

This is your fleshly nature talking. It won't easily give up control.

Therefore brokenness, as a process, is especially important. If the flesh won't easily give up control, it *must* be broken! Through this brokenness and surrender of your carnal nature, you can more easily live for God, and allow Him to flow through you to reach the world.

Let's read an excerpt from Watchman Nee's classic, 'Release of the Spirit'.

'Anyone who serves God will discover that the great hindrance to his work is not others, but himself. He will discover that his inward man (spiritual) and outward man (fleshly/carnal nature) are not in harmony, and are in fact, constantly fighting against one another. He quickly detects that the difficulty lies in this outward man, for it hinders him from using his spirit. Matthew 6:24 & Galatians 5:17.

The basic difficulty of the servant of God lies in the failure of the inward man to break through the outward man. Nothing can so hinder you as this outward man. Whether your works are fruitful or not depends on whether your outward man has been broken by the Lord so that the inward man can pass through that brokenness and come forth. When the inward man is released, both non-believers and Christians will be blessed.

John 12, "except a grain of wheat falls into the ground and die, it abides alone; but if it dies, it bears much fruit." No one would argue whether life is in the grain. But it's encased in a very hard shell. As long as the shell is unbroken, the wheat cannot sprout and grow. "Except a grain of wheat fall into the ground and die…" What is death in this parable? It's the cracking open of the shell through the working together of time, temperature, humidity etc… in the soil. Once the death takes place (the brokenness), the wheat begins to grow. So, the question is not whether there is life within, but whether the outside shell is cracked open sufficient for there to be growth.

Remember Mary's alabaster box? If the box were never to be broken, the pure spikenard could never come forth. Many still treasure the alabaster box, thinking its value exceeds the value of that of the ointment.

This becomes a problem in the Church. Some treasure their cleverness, or regard themselves better than others, some esteeming themselves as important because of their financial station or title in the Church. The subtle deceiving of your heart tricks you into not understanding that your outer man needs to be broken. Without this breaking, the inward cannot come forth. Thus, individually, you have no flowing out, and the Church does not have a living way.

The treasure is in the earthen vessels, but if the earthen vessel is not broken, who can see the treasure within? The final objective of the Lord's working in your life is to break the earthen vessel, to break the alabaster box, to crack open your shell. The Lord longs to find a way to bless the world through those who belong to Him.

Brokenness is the way of blessing, the way of fruitfulness, but it is a way sprinkled with blood. Yes, there is blood from many wounds. You *must* allow the Lord to *utterly* crack your outward man, so that He may find a way for His out-working.

You need to look back at your life and perhaps you can see that God's intention is aimed at one single objective, the breaking of the outer man. Therefore, everything that has come into your life has been meaningful. The Lord has not wasted even one thing. You must understand that all your experiences, troubles, and trials which the Lord sends you are for your highest good. So, He can live through you! You cannot expect the Lord to give better things because these are His best!

No one is more beautiful than one who is broken. What is mere knowledge of the Bible if one remains unbroken? Only the person through whom God can come forth is useful. After your outward man has been stricken, dealt with, broken, and led through many trials, you have wounds upon you. But those wounds allow the spirit to emerge. Let's look at a biblical example.

Jacob is a beautiful story of brokenness. In the O.T., Jacob struggled with his brother in his mother's womb! He was subtle, tricky, deceitful. His life was full of sorrows and grief. He ran away from home at a young age, and he was cheated for twenty years by Laban. The love of his life, Rachael, died prematurely. The son he loved, Joseph, was sold. Benjamin was detained in Egypt. He was dealt with by God, meeting misfortune after misfortune. He was stricken by God throughout his entire history!

But finally, after many such dealings, the man Jacob was transformed. In his last few years, he was quite transparent. What a beautiful picture of him worshiping on his staff! Here is one who is matured, one who knows God. Several decades of dealings have resulted in Jacob's outward man being broken. In his old age, the picture is a beautiful one.

When we really understand the Cross, we will see that it means the breaking of the outward man. The Cross reduces the outward man to death; it splits open the human shell. The Cross must break all that belongs to our outward man, our opinions, our ways, our cleverness, our self-love, our pride, our all. As soon as the outward man is broken, the inward man can easily come forth.

The Lord employs different ways to break us, some gradual, some sudden. The timing is in His hand. We cannot shorten the time, but we *can* prolong it. Stubbornness, hard-hearted, rebelliousness, etc... These hinder the work God is doing in the outward man. This may cause the potter to smash together the clay and begin anew until these characteristics are removed.

Two reasons for not being broken: First, many are not seeing the hand of God working in their lives. God is working. God is breaking but they do not recognize it as being from Him.

A second reason for not being broken: self-love.

Remember that the one reason for all misunderstanding, all fretfulness, all discontent, is that we secretly love ourselves. Thus, we devise a plan whereby we can deliver ourselves. Many times, more problems arise due to our seeking and avenue of escape—an escape from the working of the Cross.

Let no one despise the Lord's dealings. May He show us that herein is the purpose of all His dealings with us these past few months, years, or even decades! That through us, He may shine forth into the world, showing all His power and love, while simultaneously conforming us into the image of His dear Son. This is His purpose! The outward man *must* be thoroughly dealt with so that the life inside, the precious ointment, the treasure inside can come forth and bless the world with the life, the fragrance, and the treasure hidden inside each one of his children!'

What great insights into the realm of brokenness!

This is what biblical brokenness is, and its role in the life of the Christian.

God uses this process to weaken and afflict the power of the flesh, so that the life within you can come forward and touch the world. You are to go out and affect people now. Touch those inside your sphere of influence for the Glory of God! Mimic Christ in what you do, preach the Gospel, and make an eternal difference for someone!

The carnal nature will fight against you in this endeavor. But you can have the victory!

This fact that we were designed to be used by God is an important area where we get stuck in our thinking as the Church.

Our thinking tends to be carnal. It's all about Self.

Do you realize that you were *not* saved *just* so you could go to heaven? You weren't saved simply to prevent you from experiencing the fires of an eternal hell either!

So many times, heaven or hell were your focal points concerning your salvation, therefore, once you know you have achieved heaven and avoided hell, you believe nothing else is required for your life. While both gaining heaven and avoiding hell are fantastic realities for believers in Christ, they are not *why* you were saved. They are merely fringe benefits.

God paid the most precious price in the universe to secure your eternal salvation and make you a part of His family for all eternity.

"Beloved, now we are the children of God!"

You will be with Him in the everlasting future because you are part of the royal family! *That's* why we'll be in heaven, and *that's* why we'll miss hell! Those benefits came naturally as you were adopted into God's family!

But you should understand that as children of God, you are made like Him to shine in this world like Jesus did when He walked the earth.

God invested His *all* into you, and you can believe He wants a return on His investment, like anyone else! You are to go out and become salt and light to a dying world, and you don't do that by hiding that light under a bushel! But hiding, exactly the opposite of what God wants, is what the carnal nature attempts to get you to do.

Therefore, it's absolutely vital for you to understand what is happening in your life during times of brokenness events. God is doing something! He's working on you!

Understanding brokenness can help you to surrender and move forward in a positive direction during trials instead of shutting down, feeling as though God has turned against you or you've done something wrong. You can move forward, perhaps not truly appreciating what you're going through, but with a fully submitted heart, asking God what you are to learn *through* it, how are you to glorify Him while *in* it, and thanking Him for being with you to conform you to the image of Christ.

Many Christians have taken an honest look back upon brokenness events that took place within their lives and said that it was the greatest blessing God had yet bestowed upon them. After going through the trial and emerging on the other side, they found themselves stronger, more stable, and full of faith, unshakeable in the Lord and fully surrendered to Him. And their relationship with Him had only grown deeper and more fortified.

Others are watching how you handle yourself when the painful issues of life sweep over you. When they see you steadfast and unmoving concerning your faith, because you know that God is with you, using whatever trials stand ahead to conform you to the image of His Son, it brings God glory!

Many times, they ask, "How did you go through that painful time the way you did? What do you have that I don't? I've seen strong people break under the pressure that you endured, but you seemed unaffected! How?"

And an avenue opens to share the Gospel with them.

This perspective on brokenness—that it's God orchestrating your circumstances to conform you into His image, can change everything!

Through brokenness, the power of the fleshly nature is being subdued as you surrender to God's control, and the life inside of you oozes out through the cracks in your flesh to affect the world around you.

As I said before, worship and brokenness are connected.

Brokenness is God working in you to conform you into the image of Christ, by bringing you to a point of full surrender and submission. It lowers you to your basest level where you must acknowledge that you can do nothing on your own, and all you have left is to look to Him to save you. It strips you of your foolish pride and selfish ambitions. Brokenness brings you to the internal condition necessary for true worship.

When you are broken, your heart will be down low, humbled, surrendered, and reaching out with everything within you to ask Him for help.

Ps 51:17 has David saying,

"A broken spirit, a broken and contrite heart oh God, you will not despise."

David knows that God *always* draws near when one of His children is in the condition of being in pain. He comes to the rescue to hold and love them and bind up their wounds.

Therefore, brokenness, since it is a work *by* God in the process of conforming you into His image, is also the method God uses to have you cry out to Him for relief so He can come to your aid.

God becomes the initiator of the process, the Master Potter, and when you cry out from the pain of being conformed, He comes to your side, heals, and strengthens you until the next brokenness event is applied. God then, becomes all in all, the Alpha and Omega in the sanctification of your life.

As brokenness forms the heart condition, and ushers in the presence of God, worship becomes the proper response to a servant in the presence of their Lord. Through God's process, your heart becomes humbled, submitted, down low, reaching out in adoration to the lover of your soul, and as the Lord of the universe draws near to his children who cry out to Him, you prostrate yourself in homage to Him, or bow, kneel in obeisance.

This is how brokenness and worship are connected.

WORSHIP AND BROKENNESS

Worship envelops brokenness. Brokenness is the necessary first condition of worship which allows you to die, and then worship boldly ushers us enter the presence of the Almighty.

Worship is an activity you *will* yourself to do, while brokenness is an action of God *in* you and on your behalf to conform you into the image of Christ. Both take place on the Altar. Both require a death to Self. Both break the power of the flesh and allow you to commune with God in His presence. And while spending time in God's Holy presence, you can't help but change as His Spirit moves in and through you. Even when you leave the Secret Place and move out into the world, His life continues to flow from you to affect those within your sphere of influence.

This is how worship, brokenness, and the presence of God carry with you throughout everything that you do. But it's only when you are brought into the intimate presence of God and learn to abide there daily, that His loving residue stays with you.

It begins in your private time in His presence, and as you submit to God in more areas of your life, the life within you begins to flow outward until worship and brokenness(surrender) become a lifestyle. And it's in that lifestyle that you become a conduit for God blessing all who you encounter!

There's a story I once read that I fell in love with.

It describes this process of how worship and brokenness work together, just as we've been talking about.

I'd like to share it with you now.

Once upon a time in the heart of the Western Kingdom, lay a beautiful garden where in the cool of the day, the Master of the garden walked. Of all the dwellers in his garden, the most beautiful and beloved was a noble bamboo tree. Year after year, Bamboo grew yet more noble and gracious, conscious of his Master's love and watchful delight.

TRUE WORSHIP: THE GATEWAY TO INTIMACY WITH GOD

One day, the Master himself drew near to contemplate his beloved tree, and Bamboo in a passion of adoration bowed his great head to the ground.

The Master spoke: 'Bamboo, I will use you.' It seemed the day of days had come—the day for which the tree had been made!

Bamboo's voice came low and steady: 'Master, I am ready. Use me as you will.'

'Bamboo.' The Master's voice was grave. 'I must take you and cut you down.'

'Cut—me—down! Me—whom you, Master, have made the most beautiful in all your garden—cut me down? Not that; not that. Use me for your pleasure, O Master, but do not cut me down.'

WORSHIP AND BROKENNESS

'Beloved Bamboo...' The Master's voice grew graver still. 'If I do not cut you down, I cannot use you.'

The garden grew still. Wind held his breath. Bamboo slowly bent his glorious head. And Bamboo shivered in expectancy, whispering low, 'Master, if you cannot use me unless you cut me down—then—do your will and cut.' The sun hid his face. A butterfly flitted fearfully away.

'Bamboo, I would divide you in two and cut out your heart, for if I do not, I cannot use you.'

Bamboo bowed low to the ground. 'Master, then cut and divide.'

So did the Master of the garden cut Bamboo and hacked off his branches and stripped his leaves and divided him in two and cut out his heart.

Then he carried him to where there was a spring of fresh, sparkling water in the midst of the Master's dry field. There, the Master gently laid down his beloved tree. And the spring sang welcome as the clear sparkling water raced joyously down the channel of Bamboo's torn body into the thirsty waiting fields. Then the rice, and vegetables, and fruit trees were planted, and the days went by, and the shoots grew, and harvest came.

In that day, Bamboo, once so glorious, was truly put to use in his brokenness. For in his beauty, he had life abundant in himself, but in his brokenness, he became a channel of abundant life to his Master's world.

I love that story.

It accurately describes the process of brokenness, and how God uses it to bring you to surrender so you can be used by Him for a greater purpose than you could ever have had by yourself.

Unfortunately, unlike Bamboo, many don't want to submit to His control of our lives.

Here's a quote that describes this thought, "I think we are totally good to trust in Jesus for our eternity, we just don't want to hear from Him until we get there."

This is your fleshly nature talking. And as I said earlier, it won't easily give up control.

This is why brokenness, the process, is necessary!

Brokenness causes the death of self which leads to the act of surrender.

As you saw in our story of Bamboo, this surrender to God can contain a crushing of those hopes and dreams, and ideas that you deemed were good for your life, requiring an acknowledgment of that which the Master has planned for your life instead.

This can be incredibly painful.

But as Bamboo discovered, surrendering control to the Master's Plan, although vastly different than what he expected, brought a new level of use and fulfillment to the world outside himself that he never imagined!

This is a great analogy for what God can do once you are broken and fully submitted to Him.

CHAPTER SIXTEEN

WORSHIP AND DYING TO SELF

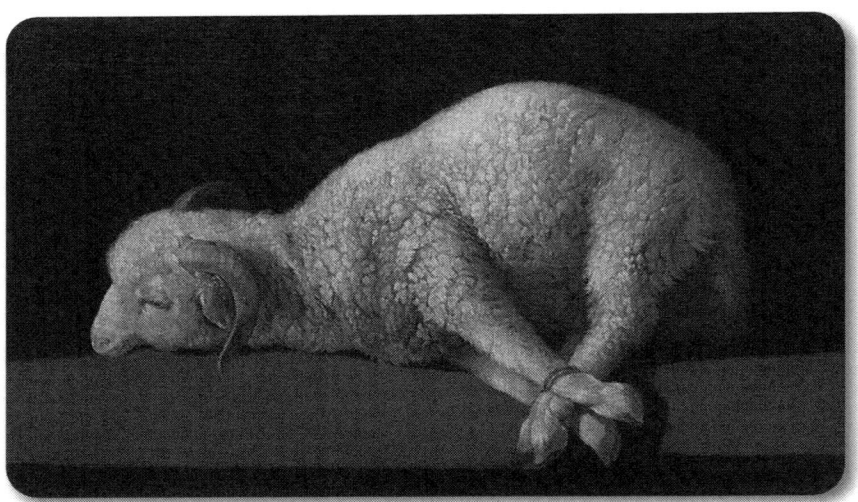

Remember our Tabernacle depiction? Through thanksgiving and praise, you move through the gates and into the courts of the Tabernacle, to be delivered to the Brazen Altar to be sacrificed.

Did I mention that *you* are the sacrifice?

Thanksgiving and praise have brought you to the place of worship, where something has to die.

TRUE WORSHIP: THE GATEWAY TO INTIMACY WITH GOD

Rom 12:1 says, "I beseech you therefore brethren, by the mercies of God, to present your bodies a living sacrifice unto God, holy and acceptable which is your reasonable service."

You are to present yourself to God, as a *living* sacrifice? What is that?

That makes no sense since you know that a sacrifice must be dead. How are you to accomplish this? How can you die, and yet still live? Worship is the willing sacrifice of self and the total surrender of the heart of all that you are, in adoration to the God of the universe.

This is *why* you are on the Altar. Self *must* die. Selfish ambitions, selfish desires, selfish pride, all your thoughts about *you* have to die!

All your dreams and goals in life must be surrendered!

And to surrender something means the death of that thing. It's no longer under *your* control, but you've forsaken it and given it over to another. Therefore, control of your life dies as you allow God to have dominance. *My* way of doing things has to be submitted to God and to *His* way. That's another death. All that you are must die on the altar. Then, and only then, can you come alive in Him! You rise from the ashes of your old life and stand in the power of the resurrected Christ within you, but you can only *fully* live to your new life in Christ once you've surrendered and died to the old. Death is what *should* happen to the old *me*.

Self *must* die or it will continue to exult itself against the new spiritual creation you have become. This has become an issue in the life of Christians in the Church. You haven't learned of the power of the flesh, or how it operates, or how to die to your carnal nature, therefore, you live lives that are always 'less than', and you never walk in the power of the Holy Spirit as God desires for you.

Please know this; in tolerating the desires of the flesh, you unwittingly learn to accommodate those same desires. Accommodation brings familiarity, and familiarity fosters comfortability. You *will* inevitably live very comfortably with the carnality of the flesh if you don't learn to utterly destroy it.

> *Matthew 6:24 says, "No man can serve two masters: for either he will hate the one and love the other; or else he will hold to the one and despise the other. Ye cannot serve God and mammon." (AKJV)*

Most of us don't see ourselves as a God. I specifically use the capital 'G' to denote the true and living God. Most of us don't equate ourselves with Him on a daily basis. At least, I hope you don't!

But did you know that in your actions, you place yourself on equal footing with the true God all the time? Every time you accept a thought or put into action what is desired by your un-surrendered carnal nature, which is opposed to what is desired by the true God, you are in effect loving your flesh and placing it alongside, *or above* your love for God.

Your flesh has then become the master you serve.

Matthew 6:24 says that you cannot serve two masters, because you'll end up hating the one and loving the other. Therefore, as you serve the desires of the flesh, are you actually loving it and hating God?

I've spoken previously about the deceitfulness of the fleshly nature, and how God has a process called brokenness to 'break' this part of you, so that you can be used for His Glory.

We've found that brokenness is the process God undertakes on your behalf to bring your carnal nature to the place of surrender.

Please hear this. Dying to self is *your* portion in the same undertaking.

It is where *you* consciously bring *yourself* under submission, killing off the desires of your flesh so that you can live for Him alone.

Our verse in Romans 12 says,

> *"I beseech you brethren, by the mercies of God, that you present your bodies a living sacrifice…"*

Paul is urging them to present their *own* bodies! It's not something he says God is supposed to do, but what *you* do in *your* service for God!

You have a part to play in dying to self! You are given responsibility in this undertaking!

Dying to self is not always easy. But you will find that when you place your carnal affections at the feet of Jesus and lay them all out fully surrendered to Him, you have arrived at the same place that true worship and brokenness bring you.

Your heart will be down low and humbled, aware of your nothingness, so He becomes everything to you. You cry out for His assistance and as He comes to your side, a renewed adoration grows in your heart. And you worship Him with all that you are, totally surrendered to His Will and His Ways.

But you will never be able to truly die to yourself if you remain comfortable living life according to your own designs. Most Christians feel living the way they have, which is according to the way of the world and the carnal nature, has brought them to the easy places they live in, so why change?

'Until we are convinced that serving the flesh (our sin nature) is totally unprofitable, we will never change. We have to see that it has absolutely no worth!'

Unfortunately, only God can change the human heart.

This is why true worship is so imperative. It places you at the feet of Jesus in the Most Holy Place in His presence, where you are able to be changed from the inside out. Your heart becomes more like His and you are better able to recognize the workings of your fleshly nature. In fact, it becomes despicable of you.

Being in His presence allows you to love the working of the Spirit taking place within. You come to love His Ways, His Holiness, His Power, His Righteousness, etc., and in the loving of one, you hate the other. In the embracing of who He is, you begin to despise all the elements of the flesh that you still contain.

Just as worship and brokenness are connected, brokenness and dying to self are similarly connected as well. One is God's endeavor on your behalf (brokenness), the other (dying to self) is your responsibility in the same endeavor.

Previously, we looked at the topic of redemption and saw that Jesus came into the world and paid for you, in horrific fashion, with His own blood, and with His own life. He then broke the bondage of sin over you and made you a slave to Himself. You no longer belong to yourself. You were bought with a price! You belong to Him! Jesus paid the price for you, and you are no longer your own.

Have you ever considered what being a slave entails?

Being a slave means you no longer own the rights to yourself!

In this pampered age of *I'm going to do whatever I want, whenever I want to do it, and you can't do anything to stop me!* the idea of slavery sounds crazy. Doesn't it?

Have you ever watched the old television mini-series 'Roots'?

Many of you may be too young to remember this landmark show when it aired on television, but when it first appeared, it was life changing. It showed in graphic detail the hurts, the pains, the whipping, the torturous lifestyle, everything concerning the life of an American slave! It hurt just watching it.

Unfortunately, when you hear the word *slave,* you identify it with the brutality of American slavery that you have had imposed on your mind.

But you must understand that having Jesus as your Master is like having the most loving person in existence, who deeply cares for your welfare, taking care of you.

The only point of reference to the brutality implied in the term *slavery,* is in how you should treat your own fleshly nature that is opposed to your new Master. It must be beaten and whipped and put down until it is killed.

A Christian slave must be dead to him or herself. That is, they must sense the opposition of their old fleshly nature that is against their new spiritual nature and put that old nature down until its desire ceases to be effective in the life of the believer.

As a slave, you do what the Master wants you to do, when He wants you to do it.

A slave no longer owns him/herself. They must be willing to forsake everything and everyone, if necessary, to give themselves in entirety to their Master.

The desires of the Master become what must be submitted to instead of the desires of one's self. As such, the individual is no longer concerned with their own will or happiness, because what they want has been placed upon the altar and sacrificed. It no longer matters.

Sounds scary, doesn't it?

To place all your hopes and dreams, everything that you are and ever hope to be in the hands of a different Master than you've known and lived for all your life?

Let's face it, most of you have lived being the master of your own little ship and never heeding anyone but yourselves. I don't say this to be harsh: it applies all of us. It's uncomfortable to step away from that and into trusting someone else to guide us through life.

We're back to faith and worship again.

It takes the utmost trust, confidence, reliance upon God and upon His Word to surrender all that we are and all that we have in humble submission and adoration before this new Master!

Throughout our study, we've seen that God's Will for our lives is that we are conformed to the image of Christ (through worship, brokenness and dying to self), and in so doing, we enjoy truly intimate fellowship with Him (through worship and faith), as He changes the world through us.

'Therefore, the secret to a "joy-filled life" doesn't lie in the absence of pain or in demanding your own way, but in dying to self and embracing God's Will.'

Dying to self obviously describes a death, or another type of surrender to Him. It's coming to the end of yourself and embracing

His way instead of *your* way. It's submitting to a brokenness of your *own* making, which always brings the Presence of God.

'Jesus described the "dying to self" process as part of the *normal* Christian life of following Him.'

> *Matthew 16:24 states, "If anyone wishes to come after Me, he must deny himself, and take up his cross and follow Me."*

'He then went on to say that "dying to self" is actually a positive, not a negative:'

> *Matthew 16:25, "For whoever wishes to save his life will lose it; but whoever loses his life for My sake will find it!"*

In dying to self, we discover the abundant life by depending upon God, who provides much more than we can imagine!

Dying to oneself involves a seeking of God's Will, which reflects the attitude of the heart. Remember, the heart is always primary. As soon as the attitude of your heart is established, the sacrificial aspect of dying to all that the flesh requires, goes away.

You *must* be motivated by a heart set on adoration. You *must* strive to obey God because you love Him for all He's done and continues to do in your life, rather than a robotic obeying of His Will over your own.

You can obey God out of fear as opposed to love, and though you obey, it will not result in lasting, life-giving benefits. The Bible says,

> *"God has not given us the spirit of fear, but of power, of love and of a sound mind."*

It also states,

> *"Fear has torment."*

You can never gain His presence by operating out of something that He has not given, but that instead brings torment, which is fear. Part of the blessed life you discover when you give your life to Christ, is freedom from a life of self-obsession. Before Christ, you never knew how much of a vile slave-master your flesh was! It is only through Christ that you are now able to view the destructive patterns of your old carnal nature and turn them over to God. In doing so, you experience the new freedom that only attends a life lived for Him.

When you die to self, you set aside your wants and desires and focus on cultivating adoration for God and valuing others more highly than yourself. Your focus, taken off yourself and placed upon loving your Creator, is what prevents your old self-centered life from taking control again and destroying your new spiritual freedom.

As stated previously, worship, brokenness and dying to self are all intertwined.

Brokenness is God's undertaking on your behalf to break the power of the carnal nature, so that you are better equipped to submit to His Will and allow His life inside of you to flow outward to affect the world, while dying to self is *your* responsibility in that same Godly endeavor of killing the flesh. It involves that portion of yourself that thinks, feels, wills, and desires to push against that which in your nature is opposed to God.

Dying to self, therefore, involves the 'in spirit' aspects of true worship.

When you don't feel like it, when you're tired, anytime the flesh says, 'I don't want to!' It brings about a fight with the fleshly nature still residing inside you. You press and strive and use that part of you that wills, thinks and decides to 'break' the fleshly grip in your life and push forward to worship Him.

Brokenness, dying to self, and worship are connected sacrificial activities that usher you into the Most Holy Place to commune with God. As worship contains surrender and death of self on the altar, and the submission of all that you are, it encompasses both concepts of brokenness and dying to self. When you worship in the manner God delights in, you are fully surrendered (broken) for God, and therefore, dead to the selfish nature within.

And through that death, His life breaks through to benefit the world around you.

Here are a few examples of men who utterly died to self, so God could be all in their lives.

George Müller, known for his great faith and ministry to orphans in 19th-century England, was asked the secret of his fruitful service for the Lord. He said, "There was a day when I died... utterly died." As he spoke, he bent lower and lower until he almost touched the floor. "I died to George Müller — his opinions, his preferences, his tastes, and his will — died to the approval or blame even of my brethren and friends — and since then I have studied only to show myself approved unto God."

Bill Bright, founder of "Campus Crusade for Christ," had this to say about "dying to self":

"Everyone I know who has been greatly used by God has gone through an experience of 'dying to self' as described in Galatians 2:20" — 'I have been crucified with Christ and I no longer live, but Christ lives in me.'" He goes on to say that it is not until you know the reality of "death to self" that you can live for Christ, allowing God to truly use and bless you. "My Galatians 2:20 experience," writes Bright, "happened in the spring of 1951 when Vonette (his wife) and I signed a contract to become 'slaves of Christ' – I daily reaffirm this contract." Holy living involves a daily decision to surrender to the "lordship of Christ." It involves yielding your will to God and adopting His perspective. If you want to see what it looks like to live a holy life, examine the life of Jesus – He is the visible expression of God's holiness. God wants your mind and heart to be filled with His holy qualities. As your lives are transformed, you will project the light of His holiness into the darkness of your evil world. Real life—abundant life—begins with dying to self. "Dying to self" is a liberating action producing joy and peace.

Noteworthy Quotes on Dying to Self

- Charles Spurgeon — 'I have now concentrated all my prayers into one... that I may die to self and live wholly to Him.'
- Martin Luther — 'Until a man is nothing, God can make nothing out of him.'
- J. I. Packer — 'Jesus Christ demands self-denial, that is, self-negation, as a necessary condition of discipleship. Self-denial is a summons to submit to the authority of God as Father and of Jesus as Lord.... Accepting death to everything that carnal self wants to possess is what Christ's summons to self-denial is all about.'
- Thomas a Kempis — 'The more a man dies to himself, the more he begins to live unto God.'
- D. L. Moody — 'Let God have your life; He can do more with it than you can.'
- Arthur Pink — 'Growth in grace... is the forming of a lower estimate of ourselves. It is a deepening realization of our nothingness.'
- Ignatius — 'Few souls understand what God would accomplish in them if they were to abandon themselves unreservedly to Him.'
- Richard Sibbes — 'Self-emptiness prepares us for spiritual fullness.'

- Richard Baxter — 'Self is the most treacherous enemy, and the most insinuating deceiver in the world. Of all other vices, it is both the hardest to find out, and the hardest to cure.'
- Vance Havner — 'Some missionaries bound for Africa were laughed at by the boat captain who said, "You'll only die over there!" Replied a missionary: "Captain, we died before we started."'
- Dr. Les Humphrey – 'If you kill the flesh, the devil doesn't have a playground.'

CHAPTER SEVENTEEN

WORSHIP: THE REALM OF MIRACLES

I would like you all to understand that as you begin to worship God truly and continually abide in His presence, you will be in the secret place of the Most High.

Scripture tells you in Psalms 91,

> *"He who dwells in the secret place of the Most High, shall abide under the shadow of the Almighty."*

When you worship the Lord, and pour out your heart to Him, His presence manifests to comfort you. This loving place is called the secret place, or under the shadow of the Almighty.

Where is His shadow?

In His intimately close presence! But it's also down low, and at His feet.

It's the place of true worship. It is a place of safety. A place of strength.

It is a place you can learn to *live* from if you truly, constantly, faithfully, accurately, and undeviatingly give God the worship that He so desires and deserves!

Let's look at a Scripture.

As Jesus entered Jerusalem, He seemed to be struck with an overwhelming sense of pain from what He knew was going to happen to the city in the future.

> *"O Jerusalem, Jerusalem, the city that kills the prophets and stones those who are sent to it! How often would I have gathered your children together as a hen gathers her brood under her wings, and you were not willing!" Matt 23:37*

He's alluding to the fact that if they had remained loyal to the God of heaven, He would have been able to gather and protect them from all danger and harm. And the picture He uses is of a mother hen protecting her young under its wings.

This is the same picture given in Psalms 91.

> *"He that dwelleth in the secret place of the most High shall abide under the shadow of the Almighty. 2 I will say of the LORD, He is my refuge and my fortress: my God; in him will I trust."*
>
> *And then in verse 4, "He shall cover thee with his feathers, and under his wings shalt thou trust: his truth shall be thy shield and buckler."*

This secret place, this place of closeness in God's presence, is where true worship takes you. It is at His feet, down low, prostrated in body and heart, and in the intimacy found by abiding in the closest proximity possible to God while on this side of eternity. The secret place is synonymous with the holiest of holies where God dwells.

And as you can see in Psalm 91, if you dwell, reside, live there with Him, nothing that means you harm can touch you!

An instance of this place of protection occurred when one of my brothers in Christ and I went to Addis Ababa, Ethiopia on a missionary trip. While many incredible things occurred during that time, I would like to focus upon one experience in particular.

One evening, we were made aware of a fireworks display that would be taking place in an area we became somewhat familiar with, called the Square. We waited until the evening and headed out toward that location.

My friend's initials start with B as do mine, so when speaking to each other, we simply called each other 'B'. B is about 6'3" tall while I am only 5'7", but both of us were about twice as wide in the shoulders as most of the Ethiopians we encountered. We wore jungle hats all the time for sun protection, but after a while, people noticed us from far off because of these distinctive hats. So, whether from the look of our hats or because of our body sizes, we were easy to pick out in a crowd.

As the night darkened, we moved farther into an open area we thought gained a good vantage point to see the fireworks. Thousands of Ethiopians were flowing into the Square, densely packing it, and offering strange but not unkind looks our way as they passed by.

It seemed they were simply curious as to who these foreigners were in their city.

We nodded and smiled and stood in place while hundreds of people slowly filed past, all hoping to find a good spot to see the fireworks.

Apparently, a wealthy sheikh who had dual heritage as an Ethiopian and a Saudi Arabian was presenting the fireworks display for the people.

They were truly amazing.

Where I live currently, the fireworks are placed on a large barge that sits out in the middle of the river and ignites the fireworks from there for the entire city to see.

In Ethiopia, they were lit from a clearing across the street from where the people stood.

Much closer proximity. Much brighter light displays. Much louder-sounding explosions!

I'm not sure how long we waited. But I remember looking up at the stars and noticing how different they looked from the heavens back home in America.

Sometime during my observance of the stars, a still small voice softly sounded inside my head saying,

"*Watch*."

I intuitively knew it was the Lord speaking to me, but I did not know what he was referring to! And my mind whirled back to recent memories that would help me discover what it was that God wanted me to be watchful for.

God is so amazing because recently before this occurrence, He had led us to do a study on the word 'watch' from the New Testament. It means, be alert, be sober, be vigilant, and the inference in my mind in this situation was that something was going to happen that I needed to be on high alert for!

All these deliberations in my mind took just a few seconds, and I knew I had to inform my brother B of what God had told me. I said, "Hey B". And in that moment, he turned and stated, "I heard it too, bro."

God spoke the same word to both of us, at the same time!

And I could see from the look on B's face was that he was searching his mind just as I was, to discover what God wanted us to watch for!

We stood silently for a time, waiting to hear any word, or guidance, or instruction from the Holy Spirit.

Have you ever been in a situation where you have a feeling someone's watching you, and the hairs on the back of your neck seem to stand up? As we waited to hear more from God, this was *exactly* what I experienced!

I *felt* someone's eyes on me, and it seemed I started to feel their intentions as well!

I *felt* an intense hatred so close behind me that I thought they may be breathing down my neck.

I turned slowly, scanning the people behind us, to see if the truth of this feeling would be confirmed.

Almost immediately, I saw him.

It looked to be a young African man with his hands clasped down in front of his body. He wore off-white-colored pants and matching tunic, but otherwise had nothing out of the ordinary to distinguish him. He stood about thirty feet away with his head down slightly, and while his posture portrayed a calm nonviolence, when our eyes met and locked, a fiery hatred was revealed.

This man wanted to kill me.

In those brief moments as our eyes remained fixed upon each other, God brought a vision before me.

I saw the fireworks going off in rapid succession across the street with blazing light and thunderous booms! And as the noise and light show commenced, I saw this man lift the front of his tunic with his left hand, revealing a silver pistol with a black handle on his waist. He grabbed and pulled the pistol out with his right hand and began walking towards us.

I could *feel* his thoughts, his intentions, his purpose!

He was set on killing two Christian missionaries at close range, while having the noise and exploding light of the fireworks cover for his deed!

As abruptly as it started, the vision stopped.

I came back to myself, noticing I was still locked eye to eye with this man.

The entire vision must have only taken a split second.

I turned back around and said, "B, there is a man directly behind us dressed in off-white. He has a pistol in the front part of his waist. When the fireworks start, he's going to walk up and kill us."

B responded simply and calmly, "OK. Let's just start moving away from him."

With the crowd still flowing in by the hundreds, we started moving out of the Square and against the flow of people. We had only taken a few steps when I turned to look again for the man in the off-white outfit. And where once there was a deadly stare of hatred and a certainty of intention to kill, now was a look of confusion! His eyes were opened wide and although we had only taken a few steps, he jerked his head from left to right, and then right at us with a blank stare!

I stopped and said, "B, look! He's looking for us, but he can't see us!"

I paused for a moment as this reality was setting in. "Are you kidding me? He *really* can't see us!"

B stopped and looked back.

I continued, "Look at his reaction!"

The man was now obviously panicked. You could see on his face that he couldn't understand where we went! He was looking in our direction, yet we were obviously nowhere to be found!

I continued, "He can't see us! This is crazy! I think we're invisible right now!"

I said, "Do you see him?" He turned to me, looked me in the eye and calmly said, "Bro, I saw him, and I saw his buddies in front of us too".

Now my mind was swimming with thoughts. There are guys in front of us who want to kill us too? This is getting crazy!

"You think *they* can see us?" I asked.

He responded calmly, "I don't know, but let's not wait around to find out."

We again began moving against the flow of the crowd, B. first, with me trailing after until we came to a place of safety. I believe I remember him telling me after we moved to a place of safety, that he looked back again and saw three men standing together still looking for us, but unable to see us even though, at that time, we *clearly* stood within their view!

They had triangulated our position and were hoping to close in upon us from all three sides, tightening the noose and preventing avenues of escape as they closed ranks.

This told me they had been trained.

Although we passed through the oncoming crowds, we were two Americans, one very tall and one shorter, both wearing distinctive jungle hats, making it impossible for anyone to overlook us.

God had covered us with His wings of protection so that all the destructive plans and training of the enemy came to naught. What happened to us was a miracle. We were *literally* invisible!

We should have been dead, but by the grace of God, we live!

It's amazing sometimes what your mind does to justify or even negate some of the miraculous things God does in your life!

At some point as we talked about the situation, I remembered that I had only told B that the man was going to take out a pistol and kill us. And for some reason, I wanted confirmation that the gun I saw in my vision was what the man actually possessed.

My mind asked, "Was that vision even real?"

I asked B, "Did you ever see the gun?" And he replied, "Yes, I saw it".

I asked him, "What did it look like?" He said, "It was a silver pistol with a black handle grip".

Finally, I could breathe a sigh of relief. "Exactly."

That confirmation settled something very deep inside me that was trying to deny this occurrence ever happened. I remember going through the incident again and again in my mind as we sat watching the fireworks, trying to recall what I felt, what I saw, what I experienced spiritually, what I felt naturally, the disbelief, the impossibility, the miracle-working power of God. It was all a jumble of heightened awareness, thinking, and sensing!

How can you adequately describe what occurs when the God of all creation enters your realm and changes the fabric of reality to keep you from harm?

Thoughts and analysis continually crossed my mind.

One realization that occurred to me afterward was, during the 'invisible' time, people still funneled past us giving us curious looks, so *they* could still see us! We must simply have been invisible to *the men* coming after us!

How does *that* work?

We were only be invisible to the ones trying to kill us!

Are you kidding me? Lord, you're amazing.

We got back to the missionary house where we stayed, and as was our habit, we fell on the floor in worship and cried out to God for His great goodness and kindness, His protection and miracle-working power.

I was still unsettled. Miracles were new to me.

The impossibility of something like this happening was weighing on me. We had become invisible to the people who had been trying to kill us.

Think about that for a moment!

First of all, someone was trying to kill me. *That* alone was a stunner!

Second, I was invisible. What a mindboggling concept!

As we got up from worshiping Him and wiped the tears from our eyes and started reading His Word, I asked God something like, "Lord, I thank you so much for what you've done. But I still need help. You've got to show me this in Scripture. What just happened?"

His response was immediate.

I opened my Bible, and the pages opened naturally to Luke 4, my eyes seeming to focus upon the following passage which then appeared to raise off the page to form in front of me:

> *Luke 4:28-40: "And all they in the synagogue, when they heard these things, were filled with wrath, 29 And rose up, and thrust him out of the city, and led him unto the brow of the hill whereon their city*

was built, that they might cast him down headlong. <u>30</u> But he passing through the midst of them went his way,"

Jesus had just spoken some truth that incensed the crowd.

They were taking Him out of the city to this high cliff to throw Him down to His death.

But something amazing happened.

It says, "…but he, passing through the midst of them went his way."

How does *that* work?

The whole crowd is trying to kill this man and He just walks off right through the middle of them?

The Scripture nonchalantly mentions it in passing, but when I read it, something touched inside my chest. I literally felt something pressing on my heart as I read this passage.

God spoke to me softly, just as He had earlier, and said, "That's what happened to you."

I have never heard this passage of Scripture taught from this context before.

Most teach on Jesus preaching in the synagogue, sitting in the Messiah's chair, what it meant to refer to Elijah and Elisha, etc. But never have I heard it taught from the context of what Jesus experienced as they dragged Him to the top of the cliff to throw Him off it.

From my experience, and from what God has told me personally, I believe Jesus either became invisible, or when they looked upon Him, they saw someone else and He was able to walk through the middle of the crowd undetected and go on His way.

Just as we did!

Incredible.

This experience is important to me because it portrays what happens when you spend time dwelling in God's secret place.

It's the place of protection and safety, the place of intimate relationship with God!

This is the resting place of true worship!

> *"He who abides in the secret place of the Most High, shall abide under the shadow of the Almighty"*
> *Psalms 91:1*

When you worship Him truly, He comes to your side and you enjoy a lovefest of activity with the Most High God! No demon in hell can come near to harm you while you're at rest in that intimate place of God's Presence!

There are many other incredible spiritual experiences I would like to share.

But this is *your* journey!

You and the Lord will create unbelievable times of intimacy, miracles, life lessons etc., as your relationship with Him grows.

My Pastor revealed experiences and miracles that the Lord performed through him that still to this day, blow my mind. But I needed to hear them to know that they were possible.

God *still* does the impossible! God *still* performs miracles!

Now *you* know it too.

Now *you* can grow closer to Him in faith that He will reveal Himself to you in incredible ways that you and He share as well.

Some of you needed to hear about these miracles of God for no other reason except that you now know they can happen to you too, so start trusting in God with all your heart!

Worship Him with everything you have within you and watch your relationship with Him grow strong.

Then start recording His great and wonderful works in your life!

Someone within your sphere of influence will need to hear what God is doing *through you* and be encouraged and strengthened in faith to believe God for miraculous experiences in their own lives as well.

CHAPTER EIGHTEEN

TRUE WORSHIP: THE GATEWAY TO INTIMACY WITH GOD

One of the most alarming things about the Church in America is that we are so comfortable in our lackluster relationship with the Lord and complacent in our spiritual perspectives concerning Him, that we have no idea when we are totally missing the mark.

TRUE WORSHIP: THE GATEWAY TO INTIMACY WITH GOD

Unfortunately, worship is one such area.

Therefore, in that complacency, we don't long for deeper relationship with God. We don't seek Him with all our hearts. We don't fast and pray to get rid of the power of our flesh and gain greater understanding of what God wants for our lives.

We're not desperate for more of Him.

We need the fire of God's Presence to inundate and overwhelm us until we long for nothing but Him!

It's in *this* life that we are preparing for eternity! You've already seen what is taking place in heaven at this moment. It is worship without end! *Every* being, great and small, *will* worship Him in the way He desires!

The Bible says,

> *"Every knee shall bow, and every tongue shall confess that Jesus Christ is Lord to the glory of God the Father."*

We *will* all worship him one day!

Today can be the start of something brand-new in your life. You can begin right now to have the intimate relationship with God that your perfect spiritual man/woman inside you is crying out for, that God is desiring, and that can bring forth the power of God through your life to touch all those around you!

The world is dying! Every man has gone astray and done what is right in his own eyes, which has taken him further away from the Lord.

Meanwhile, the Church has lost its voice. That voice must return and become prominent in the world again!

God is beginning to open the eyes of His people to allow them to see the truth of what true worship is, why He desires it, and how He reacts when receiving it.

God is bringing about a new breed of man/woman!

A breed founded upon the understanding of who they are in Christ and what they can become when fully intimate with Him.

Never before in history has it been more necessary for those of you who know the truth of God's Word and understand the implications of what it means to truly worship, to put that knowledge into practice and boldly enter into His presence.

Now is the time to do it. The world is in disarray. It's growing more disturbed, confused, and therefore more ungodly every day! Sickness and diseases are running rampant and causing fear to have the torment the Bible says it brings!

But it doesn't have to be this way!

You can be the change in the world you want to see.

Cry out for your friends and family! Come before God on behalf of those who are within your sphere of influence. He can change their lives for all eternity!

But we've got to get the distractions out of the way.

In most cases, our eyes and ears are more tuned into the major television stations, or Facebook, Twitter, Instagram and other social media outlets, than they are toward God and what *He's* doing. We're spending more time on the internet reading about the latest news developments, than we are reading God's Word.

Therefore, our perspective has become jaded. We have become cynical, thinking that God isn't going to do anything. And some might even unconsciously adopt the same mindset the world has, which is one of depression and hopelessness.

This all has to change!

God is going to have a people! This new breed will be a people of His heart. They will walk in the intimacy of His presence. And because they seek Him privately, He will reward them openly. These are the ones who walk with God so closely that they will exude His power as easily as they breathe!

And it will all start with true worship, which gains you the intimacy of His personal presence and the benefits derived from abiding in that presence.

You don't need more intellectual understanding of the Scriptures if it's not accompanied by an experiential living in the presence of the One who encapsulates those Scriptures!

What does more knowledge obtain? The Bible says that knowledge puffs up. And it's exactly true. You learn and learn and become more knowledgeable and intellectual until all your theological degrees earn you the right to have more letters behind your name than anyone else. Believers hold you in high esteem, and you're given positions of authority within the Church, and all the while you have never ventured close enough to enter into God's intimate presence.

What a travesty!

Christians, pastors and congregants, seminarians and theologians need to know there's so much more that they can have in Christ!

You *all* need to know how God longs for you to search for Him! He says, when you seek Him, you *will* find Him.

If you could have your spiritual eyes opened for a moment to see the almost desperate desire God has to bring you closer to Himself, to hold you, coddle you, protect you from all harm, whisper revelation in your ears, lead you and guide you into all truth and provide a future and a destiny for you to grow into right here, before you ever leave this life for eternity, it would change you forever!

I pray these are the things that you have gleaned while reading through these pages.

I pray you all understand now that *everything* changes when your heart changes.

You've learned that what's inside has to come out. When your heart has been inundated with the loving Presence of the Almighty God, and you have learned to reside with Him, His overwhelming presence is carried with you wherever you go. And through the wounds still visible throughout your carnal nature from brokenness events, the very life of God flows outward from inside of you to reach a dying world.

God, we need You to change us! We need You to place a burning desire in our hearts! Please perform a work in us that begins to develop that longing for more of You! Lord, the most difficult prayer to pray is, 'Not my will, but Your Will be done.' I pray that prayer right now for each and every person reading these words. Do what is necessary to bring us closer to You! Break us, God! Crush our sense of self-righteousness, our pride, our self-centeredness, and make us more like You! Conform us, Lord, to the image of Your Dear Son! We need you! And we will in turn, pour out our hearts to You, knowing You always draw near to Your children that are hurting! And as we enter Your Presence, we will humbly bow down, lifting You up with the utmost respect, the highest honor, and the dearest adoration of our hearts to give You that one thing that You've been seeking from us all along. Thank you so much Lord. We trust that You will accomplish all this in and through us as we worship You.

God so longs for intimate communion with you.

Do you now realize that there is a deeper relationship God has for you after salvation?

He's given many of you glimpses into the spiritual realm, or experiences that have overwhelmed you with who He is, to allow you to see that there is much more of Him that you can have access to.

You've gained understanding of exactly what God is seeking, and why He's seeking it. Our own amplified version of that Scripture from John 4:23-24 reads like this:

> *But the hour cometh, and now is, when the true (the faithful, the constant – or all the time, accurate – which is perfectly according to the standard, correct, and undeviating – or never moving from the proper path) worshipers (adorers of God, those who hold the deepest respect, the highest honor, and love Him with*

all their hearts, and souls, and minds) shall worship (bow themselves down in humble submission, kneel or prostrate themselves publicly with their body and hearts in subjection to God, orally declaring the great love they have toward) the Father in spirit (that part of them that thinks, feels, wills, and desires) and in truth: for the Father seeks (is looking for, desiring, bending His efforts toward trying to find) such to worship Him. (vs 24) God is a Spirit (He's pure essence, not composed of material parts, but a pure and Holy Spirit essentially); and they that worship Him must (it's mandatory. If you're going to worship Him, it's mandatory that you do it in this way!) worship Him in spirit and in truth (the always accurate and undeviating – wherever you are and in whatever circumstances you find yourself – the Word of God).

This is what He's seeking!

And *that* knowledge taught you how you can enter into God's presence to build your relationship, make it stronger until you, like John the disciple whom Jesus loved, can lie reclining on Jesus' bosom on a daily basis, loving Him and receiving His love and revelation in return.

It's only after becoming truly intimate with Him, that you then discover how God releases Himself *through* you to touch the world around you.

What a truly awesome process!

This includes God's Divine method for breaking the power of the flesh in your life so that you may be used to fulfill His Will. And then you experience the incredible power that comes when His manifested presence enters your reality to bless you and the Church.

God has done and will continue to do amazing things in you and through you if you would only allow Him.

Please hear me.

This is not to be taken lightly.

Too many Christians hear a Word from God or read of God-given revelations, enjoy the brief respite from the norm it brings, then go back to living exactly the way they were before the Word/revelation was given.

No more!

Times are quickly approaching when you will *have* to be intimately close to the Lord!

The testing of your faith is coming.

You don't have the strength to stand against the flood of adversity that's about to overwhelm you! What we've seen lately is not even the tip of the iceberg!

Getting and staying close to Jesus is your *only* hope!

Learn to run into the secret place of the Most High, where He will shelter you from all danger. He gives you His Word which *cannot* be broken.

You have an actual promise from the God of the universe that when you seek Him with all your heart, you will find Him! And when you find Him, you will have joy unspeakable and full of glory! You can rest in peace and safety under His protection. And all the world around you will be blessed as you become a conduit for the Life of God within you to be released for their benefit.

It all starts when you enter that portal of protection, the gateway to intimacy: true worship.

Are you ready?

Let's begin.

REFERENCES

"True Worship: The Gateway to Intimacy with God" contains theological study materials and biblically researched references, along with quotes and excerpts from the following sources:

1. The Holy Bible: Most Scriptural references were taken from the King James Version of the Bible. References from the (ESV) English Standard Version (online), the Companion Bible (KJV) Kregel Publications 1990, and Dake's Annotated Reference Bible (copyright 1963, 1991) were consulted as well.
2. Main theological content derived from: "The Worship Sheet", by Dr. Les Humphrey ('Pops').
3. Strong's Exhaustive Concordance, Thomas Nelson Publishers 1990.
4. Thayer's Greek Lexicon, Hendrickson Publishers; Reissue, Subsequent edition (August 1, 1995).
5. Websters Dictionary of the English Language 1828 Version (online).
6. Vines Expository Dictionary of Old and New Testament Words, Thomas Nelson Publishers 1984, 1996.
7. Roget's Thesaurus of Synonyms and Antonyms (online).
8. Barnes Notes on the New Testament, Kregel Classics; 8th edition (June 30, 1962).

REFERENCES

9. Illustrated Manners and Customs of the Bible, Copyright 1990, Thomas Nelson Publishers.
10. Release of the Spirit, Watchman Nee, Copyright ©2000 Christian Fellowship Publishers, Inc. New York.
11. Benefits of Brokenness Part 1, and 2; (blog) www.RefineUs.org; Justin and Trish Davis; http://refineus.org/benefits-of-brokenness-part-1/
12. God, Make Us Desperate! Article by Jon Bloom, Staff writer, www.desiringGod.org, https://www.desiringgod.org/articles/god-make-us-desperate
13. Urgent Adoration excerpts and concepts from message, Jim Drake, contributed Feb 27, 2008, www.sermoncentral.com https://www.sermoncentral.com/sermon-series/7-weeks-of-urgency-sermon-series-from-jim-drake-586
14. Dying to Self, from the Transformed Soul, online, Dr. D.W. Ekstrand, sermoncentral.com, http://www.thetransformedsoul.com/additional-studies/spiritual-life-studies/dying-to-self
15. Images taken from Free Google Images https://images.google.com/ and Unsplash.com https://unsplash.com/s/photos

Made in the USA
Las Vegas, NV
16 February 2021